INSIDERS'GUIDE®

hostels series

hostels ireland

the only comprehensive, unofficial, opinionated guide

Third Edition

D0451382

paul karr

INSIDERS'GUIDE®

GUILFORD, CONNECTICUT
AN IMPRINT OF THE GLOBE PEQUOT PRESS

acknowledgments

Thanks to the tireless freelance contributors, who were our eyes and ears and mostly preferred to remain anonymous so that they can continue hostelling undisturbed.

Thanks to Hostelling International's U.S. and Irish offices for continuous encouragement and assistance; to the independent hostel organizations of Ireland, among the best anywhere; and anyone else who provided information, shelter, or a kind word.

And thanks, finally, to a world (literally) of new friends met or made on the road.

thank you all.

INSIDERS'GUIDE®

Copyright © 1999, 2001, 2004 by Paul Karr

Text design by M. A. Dubé
Editorial assistance by Evan Halper
Contributors: Jim Kennedy and Wendy Wyatt
Photos courtesy of Shiplake Mountain Hostel and Independent Holiday Hostels of Ireland
Maps by XNR Productions Inc. © The Globe Pequot Press

ISSN 1547-4895
ISBN 0-7627-2994-5

Manufactured in the United States of America
Third Edition/First Printing

contents

ireland

Ballycastle

NORTHERN
IRELAND
(U.K.)

Belfast

NORTHWESTERN
IRELAND

Belmullet

Newcastle

Boyle

Ardee

Westport

Longford

Ceanannus
Mor

Claremorris

Clifden

Kinnegad

DUBLIN

Galway

WESTERN
IRELAND

EASTERN
IRELAND

Aran
Islands

Ennistimon

Ennis

Roscrea

Limerick

Kilkenny

Cahir

Wexford

Dingle

Mallow

Killarney

Dungarvan

SOUTHWESTERN
IRELAND

Cork

Youghal

Kinsale

Skibbereen

contents

The prices and rates listed in
this guidebook were con-
firmed at press time. We
recommend, however, that
you call establishments
before traveling to obtain
current information.

key to icons

Attractive natural setting

Ecologically aware hostel

Superior kitchen facilities or cafe

Offbeat or eccentric place

Superior bathroom facilities

Romantic private rooms

Comfortable beds

A particularly good value

Wheelchair accessible

Good for business travelers

Especially well suited for families

Good for active travelers

Visual arts at hostel or nearby

Music at hostel or nearby

Great hostel for skiers

Bar or pub at hostel or nearby

 Editors' choice: among our very favorite hostels

how to use
this book

What you're holding in your hands is the first-ever attempt of its kind: a comprehensive listing and rating of hostels in Ireland. Dozens of hostellers from countries all over the globe were interviewed in the course of putting this guide together, and their comments and thoughts run throughout its pages. Who knows? You, yourself, might be quoted somewhere inside.

We wrote this guide for two pretty simple reasons: First, we wanted to bring hostelling to a wider audience. Hostels continue to grow in popularity, but many North American travelers still don't think of them as options when planning a trip. We wanted to encourage that because—at its best—the hostelling experience brings people of greatly differing origins, faiths, and points of view together in a convivial setting. You learn about these people, and also about the place in which the hostel is situated, in a very personal way that no textbook could ever provide.

Second, we wanted very much to give people our honest opinions of the hostels. You wouldn't send your best friend to a fleabag, and we don't want readers traveling great distances only to be confronted with filthy kitchens, nasty managers, or dangerous neighborhoods. At least, we thought, we could warn them about unsafe or unpleasant situations ahead of time.

Of course we would also tip our friends off to the truly wonderful hostels—the ones with treehouses, cafes, free breakfasts, and real family spirit. So that's what we've done. Time after time on the road we have heard fellow travelers complaining that the guidebooks they bought simply listed places to stay but didn't rate them. Well, now we've done it—and we haven't pulled a single punch or held back a bit of praise.

how we wrote this book

The author, along with a cadre of assistants, fanned out across Ireland with notebooks and laptops in hand during 1999, 2000, and 2003. Sometimes we identified ourselves in advance as authors; sometimes we just popped in for surprise visits. We counted rooms, turned taps, tested beds. And then we talked with managers and staff.

Before we left we also took the time to interview plenty of hostellers in private and get their honest opinions about the places they were staying or had already stayed.

The results are contained within this book: actual hosteller quotes, opinions, ratings, and more.

what is a hostel?

If you've picked up this book, you probably know what a hostel is. On the other hand, a surprising number of people interviewed for this book weren't sure at all what it means.

So let's check your knowledge with a little pop quiz. Sharpen your pencils, put on your thinking caps, then dive in.

1. A hostel is:
   A. a hospital.
   B. a hospice.
   C. a hotel.
   D. a drunk tank.
   E. none of the above.

(correct answer worth 20 points)

2. A hostel is:
   A. a place where international travelers bunk up.
   B. a cheap sleep.
   C. a place primarily dedicated to bunks.
   D. all of the above.

(correct answer worth 20 points)

3. You just turned 30. Word on the street has it that you'll get turned away for being that age. Do you tell the person at the hostel desk the grim news?
   A. No, because a hostel is restricted to students under 30.
   B. No, because a hostel is restricted to elderly folks over 65.
   C. No, because they don't care about your midlife crisis.

(correct answer worth 10 points)

4. You spy a shelf labeled free food! in the hostel kitchen. What do you do?
   A. Begin stuffing pomegranates in your pockets.
   B. Ask the manager how food ended up in jail.
   C. Run for your life.

(correct answer worth 5 points)

5. Essay question. Why do you want to stay in a hostel?

(extra credit; worth up to 45 points)

Done? Great! And the envelope, please . . .

1. **None of the above.** The word *hostel* is German, and it means "country inn for youngsters" or something like that. In French, it's called an *auberge de jeunesse*, and in Italy, it's called an *ostello*; if you ever get lost, look for signs with those words on them.

2. **All of the above**. You got that one, right?

3. **C.** No age limits or restrictions here!

4. **A.** Free means free.

5. Give yourself 15 points for every use of the word "friends," "international," or "cool," okay? But don't give yourself more than 45. Yes, we mean it. Don't make us turn this car around right now. We will. We mean it.

What? All you wrote was "It's cheap"? Okay, okay, give yourself 20 points.

So how did you do?

100 points:	Born to be wild
80–99:	Get your motor runnin'
40–79:	Head out on the highway
21–39:	Lookin' for adventure
0–20:	Hope you don't come my way

Don't be embarrassed if you flunked this little quiz, though. Hostel operators get confused and blur the lines, too. You'll sometimes find a campground or retreat center or college setting aside a couple bunks—and calling itself a hostel anyway. In those cases we've used our best judgment about whether a place is or isn't a hostel.

Also, we excluded some joints—no matter how well-meaning—if they (a) exclude men or women, (b) serve primarily as a university residence hall (with a very few special exceptions), or (c) serve you a heavy side of religious doctrine with the eggs in the morning.

In a few cases our visits didn't satisfy us either way; those places were left out, set aside for a future edition, or briefly described here but not rated.

understanding the ratings

All the information in this book was current as of press time. Here's the beginning of a sample entry in the book, from a hostel in Dublin (that's in eastern Ireland).

four courts hostel

15–17 Merchants Quay, Dublin
Phone Number: 01–672–5839

Fax number: 01–672–5862
E-mail: info@fourcourtshostel.com
Web site: www.fourcourtshostel.com
Rates: €15–€27 per person (about $15–$27 US), doubles
€55–€66 (about $55 US–$66 US)
Beds: 230
Private/family rooms: Yes
Kitchen available: Yes
Office hours: Twenty-four hours
Affiliation: None
Extras: Internet access, laundry, bureau de change, lounge, game
room, pool tables, tour desk, breakfast

See that little picture at the bottom of the listing? That's an icon, and it signifies something important we wanted you to know about the hostel. We've printed a key to these icons on page vi.

The overall hostel rating consists of those hip-looking thumbs sitting atop each entry. It's pretty simple: Thumbs up means good. Thumbs down means bad.

We've used these thumbs to compare the hostels to one another; only a select number of hostels earned the top rating of one thumb up, and a few were considered unpleasant enough to merit a thumb down. You can use this rating as a general assessment of a hostel.

Often we didn't give any thumbs at all to a hostel that was a mixed-bag experience. Or maybe, for one reason or another—bad weather, bad luck, bad timing, remoteness, an inability to get ahold of the staff, or our own confusion about the place—we just didn't feel we collected enough information to properly rate that hostel for you.

That said, here's a key to what these ratings mean:

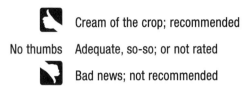

Cream of the crop; recommended

No thumbs   Adequate, so-so; or not rated

Bad news; not recommended

The rest of the information is pretty much self-explanatory:

Address is usually the hostel's street address; occasionally we add the mailing address if it's different from the street address.

Phone is the primary phone number.

Fax is the primary fax number.

E-mail is the staff's e-mail address, for those who want to get free information or book a room by computer.

Web site indicates a hostel's World Wide Web page address.

Rates are the cost per person to stay at the hostel—expect to pay somewhere around €10 to €15 (about $10 to $15 US) per person as a rule, more in cities or popular tourist areas. For private or family rooms, we've listed the total price for two people to stay in the room; usually it's higher than the cost of two singles, sometimes considerably so. Single or triple room rates will vary; ask ahead if you're unsure what you'll pay.

Note that these rates sometimes vary by season, or by membership in a hostelling group such as Hostelling International (HI); we have tried to include a range of prices where applicable. Most HI member hostels, for instance, charge a little extra if you don't belong to one of Hostelling International's worldwide affiliates.

Also, some hostels charge a small amount to supply sheets and towels if you haven't brought your own. (Sleeping bags, no matter how clean you think they are, are often frowned upon.) Finally, various local, municipal, or other taxes might also add to the rates quoted here.

Credit cards can be a good way to pay for a bed in a foreign country (you get the fairest exchange rates on your home currency). More and more hostels are taking them. If credit cards are accepted, we have noted this here. That usually means Visa and MasterCard, less often American Express as well. Call the hostel for specific information. If no credit line appears, that means that none were accepted at the time we did our research, but things may have changed. Again, call ahead and ask if you plan to use a card.

Beds is the total number of beds in a hostel (double beds we've counted as two beds).

Private/family rooms are rooms for a couple, a family with children, or (sometimes) a single traveler. Sometimes it's nice to have your own room on the road: It's more private, more secure, and your snoring won't bother anyone. Most Irish hostels—especially the independent ones—offer at least one private room, often the most atmospheric or romantic room in the joint. Private rooms are hard to get, especially in summer; call way in advance if you know you want one.

Kitchen available indicates whether or not the hostel maintains a kitchen for hostellers.

Office hours indicate the hours when staff are at the front desk and answer the phones, or at least would consider answering the phones. (Although European custom is to use military time—and all bus and train schedules read that way—most Irish hostel managers talk like Americans and say 11:30 for 11:30 P.M., not 23:30. We've used "American" time throughout this book.)

Keep in mind that nothing is ever fixed in stone; some hostel staffs will happily field calls in the middle of the night if you're reasonable, while others can't stand it. Try to call within the listed hours if possible. A good rule to follow: The smaller a place, the harder it is for the owner/manager to drag him/herself out of bed at four in the morning just because you lost your way. Big-city hostels, however, frequently operate just like hotels—somebody's always on duty, or at least on call.

Season indicates what part of the year a hostel is open—if it's closed part of the year. (Since this hostel has no "Season" line, that means it's open year-round.) We've made our best effort at listing the seasons of each hostel, but schedules sometimes change according to weather or a manager's vacation plans. Call if you're unsure whether a hostel will be open when you want to stay there.

Affiliation indicates whether a hostel is affiliated with Hostelling International or any of several smaller hostel groups. For more information about what these organizations do, see "A Word About Affiliations" (page 10).

Extras list some of the other amenities that come with a stay at the hostel. Some—but not all—will be free; there's an amazing variety of services, and almost as big a variety in managers' willingness to do nice things for free. Laundries are almost never free, and there's usually a charge for meals (which we've indicated by a dollar sign), lockers, bicycle or other equipment rentals, and other odds and ends. On the other hand, some hostels maintain free information desks. Some give you free meals, too.

Lockout and **Curfew.** Many hostels have hours during which you are locked out of the place (in other words, you're not permitted on the premises). Many also have a curfew; be back inside before this time, or you'll be locked out for the night.

With each entry, we've also given you a little more information about the hostel, to make your stay a little more informed—and fun. This sidebar shows the last part of the hostel entry that began above.

Gestalt:
Courts and Sparks

Hospitality:
Cleanliness:
Party index:

What does all that stuff mean?

Gestalt is the general feeling of a place, our (sometimes humorous) way of describing what it's about.

Safety describes urban hostels only. We grade based on both the quality of the neighborhood and the security precautions taken by the hostel staff, using this scale:

No worries

Keep an eye out

Dial 911

Hospitality rates the hostel staff's friendliness toward hostellers (and travel writers).

Smile city

Grins & growls

Very hostile hostel

Cleanliness rates, what else, the general cleanliness of a place. Bear in mind that this can change—rapidly—depending on the time of year, turnover in staff, and so forth. Use it only as a general guide.

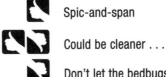

Spic-and-span

Could be cleaner . . .

Don't let the bedbugs bite

The **party index** is our way of tipping you off about the general scene at the hostel:

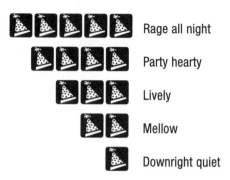

Rage all night

Party hearty

Lively

Mellow

Downright quiet

In certain writeups, we've added even more information:

Best bet for a bite tells you where to find food in the area; usually, we'll direct you to the cheapest and closest supermarket. But sometimes, in the interest of variety—and good eatin'—we'll point you toward a health food store, a place rich with local color, or even a fancy place.

Insiders' tip is a juicy secret about the area, something we didn't know until we got to the hostel ourselves.

What hostellers say relates what hostellers told us about a hostel —or what we imagine they would say.

Finally, **How to get there** includes directions to many hostels—by car, bus, train, plane, or even ferry, in some cases. Subway directions are given in big cities if applicable. Often these directions are complicated, however; in those cases, managers have asked (or we recommend) that you call the hostel itself for more precise directions.

a short history
of hostelling

Hostelling as we know it started around 1907, it started around 1907, when Richard Schirmann, an assistant schoolteacher in Altena, Germany, decided to make one of the empty classrooms a space for visiting students to sleep. That was not a completely unique idea, as Austrian inns and taverns had been offering reduced rates and bunk space to students since 1885. But Schirmann would develop much grander plans. He was about to start a movement.

His idea was to get students out of the industrial cities and into the countryside. Schirmann was a strong believer that walking and bicycling tours in the fresh air were essential to adolescent development and learning. But such excursions were impossible without a place to spend the night. His logic was simple: Since rural schoolhouses were deserted during weekends and holidays, why not make use of those spaces?

The caretakers of the school he chose agreed to serve as houseparents, and some fast ground rules were established. Students were responsible for piling up the tables and benches in the classroom and laying out thin straw sacks on the floor. At some ungodly early-morning hour, the students were to stack the straw mats back up and organize the classroom back as they found it. Boys and girls slept in separate rooms but were treated as equals. Detractors cried scandal, wondering aloud what was going on in these schoolrooms after dark.

The experiment worked, sort of. Altena became a haven for student excursions into the countryside, but finding shelter in other communities proved to be difficult. Sometimes the situation would become dire. Late one night in the summer of 1909, Schirmann decided it was time to expand his movement beyond Altena. His goal was to establish a network of hostels within walking distance of one another; beginning in a schoolhouse with straw mats, Schirmann eventually acquired the use of a castle. It still stands—the Ur-hostel, if you will—in Altena, and it's still used as a hostel.

After World War I the movement really began to spread. By 1928 there were more than 2,000 hostels worldwide. Today tens of thousands of hostellers stay at HI-affiliated hostels each year, hailing from everywhere from Alaska to Zaire; thousands more stay at independent hostels.

Hostels aren't always located within a day's walk of one another, though in parts of Ireland—like the Southwest, where a single tiny town might have ten hostels—they are, and many people do indeed walk from hostel to hostel with just a pack on their back. In any case, you're quite likely to find a promising brew of cultural exchange and friendship over pots of ramen noodles and instant coffee almost anywhere you go.

In that sense, perhaps, Richard Schirmann's dream has been realized after all.

a word about affiliations

A majority of hostels in this book are affiliated with Hostelling International (HI); the rest, we've labeled independent hostels.

An Oige (AO) is the small Irish branch of Hostelling International, long the backbone of hostelling worldwide. This organization is part of the International Youth Hostel Federation, which has 5,000 member hostels in seventy countries. Member hostels are held to a number of regulations, such as maximum number of beds per shower, even a minimum amount of space that must exist between top bunks and the ceiling. A membership in HI is usually required to stay in these hostels, but you can usually purchase a year's membership right at the hostels.

The organization's mission statement trumpets its contribution to "the education of young people," so be warned that some of its most popular hostels attract youth groups like molasses does flies. Families and senior travelers are also attracted to the Hostelling International network in increasing numbers. Bottom line: They can be extremely boring. Like going back to school—or, in the worst cases, prison.

Back to the rules. Liquor is supposed to be off-limits at most of these places, and guests tend to be an orderly bunch. Many of the giant urban hostels are purpose-built facilities owned by the organization itself, often resembling well-equipped college dormitories. Some of these HI-owned hostels have developed impressive educational programs that incorporate volunteers from the local community and so forth.

In Ireland, only about forty hostels belong to this network.

Independent Holiday Hostels (IHH) is a much larger group, four times bigger in fact, and these places are generally so good that they make Ireland one of the few countries in the world where independent hostels are actually better quality than the HI-affiliated joints. IHH generally maintains very high-quality hostels—laid-back and fun but clean, usually in really funky buildings such as mills, mansions, or farmhouses. Some have banquet halls serving wonderful dinners.

Idyllic country location for a barrel-top caravan at Shiplake
Mountain Hostel
Dunmanway, Co. Cork
(Photo courtesy of Shiplake Mountain Hostel)

The Independent Hostel Organization (IHO) is a newer group of hostels scattered throughout Ireland. Again, rules are fewer, and there's more of an emphasis on rural farmhouse and simple-type accommodations than with either An Oige or IHH.

A few hostels in Ireland have no affiliation whatsoever. Some owners simply opt not to join because membership costs are high, and they feel the return on such an investment isn't enough. Such a decision—in and of itself—does not reflect on the quality of the hostel. It would be foolish to write a hostel off simply because it is not affiliated. On the other hand, there's no guarantee of quality, and the standards, upkeep, noise level, and beer flow tend to vary widely from place to place.

Hostelling International Northern Ireland (HINI) is the Hostelling International affiliate in Northern Ireland; you'll notice a handful of those joints in the Northern Ireland chapter at the end of this book.

how to
hostel

Hostelling is, generally speaking, easy as pie. Plan ahead a bit and use a little common sense, and you'll find check-in goes pretty smoothly.

reserving a bed

Getting a good bunk will often be your first and biggest challenge, especially if it's high season. Hostellers often have an amazingly laissez-faire attitude about reservations; many simply waltz in at midnight expecting a bed will be available.

Sometimes it is. Sometimes it isn't.

Most every Hostelling International abode takes advance reservations of some form or another, so if you know where you're going to be, use this service. Increasingly, the popular Irish hostels make you confirm your booking the day before if you didn't hold the bed with a credit-card deposit. Make sure you call! Or you'll lose that bunk.

Some HI hostels are also affiliated with the worldwide International Booking Network; check with a big HI hostel and you might be able to book future dates at smaller ones.

Independent hostels are sometimes more lax about taking solid reservations, though they're also a lot more willing to find extra couch space or a spare mattress in case you're squeezed out. Calling a few days ahead to feel the situation out is always a good idea.

If you can't or won't reserve, the best thing to do is get there super-early. Office opens at 8:00 A.M.? Get there at 7:00. No room, but checkout ends at 11:00? Be back at 11:05 in case of cancellations or unexpected checkouts. The doors are closed again til 4:30 in the afternoon? No problem. Come back around 4:00 with a paperback and camp out on the porch. That's your only shot if you couldn't or wouldn't reserve ahead, and hostellers are pretty respectful of the pecking order: It really is first come, first served. So come first.

paying the piper

Once you're in, be prepared to pay for your night's stay immediately—before you're even assigned a bunk. Take note ahead of time which hostels take credit cards, checks, and so forth. Think you're being cheated with the bill? Remember that most hostels charge up to €1.00 (about $1.00 US) per night for linens if you haven't brought your own. (You always have the option of bringing your own, however, and we recommend it.)

Other charges could include a surcharge for a private room and charges for phone calls from your room, if a phone is included (very unusual).

You might also need to leave a small deposit for your room key—usually about $5.00 US, sometimes more—which you'll get back when you check out, unless you lost the key in the meantime. Sometimes you will also be required to show some form of photo identification to check in. Very occasionally, you'll even be forced to leave a passport or driver's license with the front desk. This is annoying and possibly illegal, but a few hostels still get away with it. Scream bloody murder; threaten to sue—but you might still get shut out unless you play along.

Remember to pay ahead if you want a weekly stay. Often you can get deep discounts, though the downside is that you'll almost never get a partial refund if you decide you can't stand it and leave before the week is up.

If you're paying by the day, rebook promptly each morning; hostel managers are very busy during the morning hours, keeping track of check-ins, checkouts, cleaning duties, and cash. You'll make a friend if you're early about notifying them of your plans for the next day. Managers hate bugging guests all morning or all day about whether they'll be staying on. Don't put the staff through this.

Some hostel managers have the curiously softhearted habit of letting the rent slide a few days. We can't figure why; when managers do this, a day often becomes a week or a month. Even if this courtesy is extended to you, don't accept it except in an emergency. You never know who they'll hire to get that money out of you later.

All right, so you've secured a bed and paid up. Now you have to get to it. This may be no easy task at some hostels, where staff and customers look and act like one and the same. A kindly manager will probably notice you bumbling around and take pity. As you're being shown to your room, you're also likely to get a short tour of the facilities and a briefing on the ground rules.

knowing the ground rules

There's one universal ground rule at every hostel: You are responsible for serving and cleaning up after yourself. And there's a corollary rule:

Be courteous. So while you're welcome to use all the kitchen facilities, share the space with your fellow guests—don't spread your five-course meal all over the counter space and rangetop burners if other hungry folks are hanging around waiting. And never, ever, leave a sink full of dirty pots and pans behind. That's bad form.

Hostel guests are almost always asked to mark their name and check-in date on all the food they put in the refrigerator. Only the shelf marked free food is up for grabs; everything else belongs to other hostellers, so don't touch it. (Hostellers get very touchy about people stealing their grub.) Some of the better-run hostels have a spice rack and other kitchen essentials on hand. If you're not sure whether something is communal, ask. But don't assume anything is up for grabs unless it is clearly marked as such.

Alcohol is still a major issue at some hostels. Hostelling International rules officially forbid it on the premises of HI hostels. We were not surprised to see this rule bent or broken in some places, but inquire with a smile on your face before you bring that brew inside. Independent hostels are a lot more forgiving; some even have bars.

Then there's the lockout, a source of bitter contention among hostel factions. A few rural and small-city Hostelling International hostels throw everybody out in the morning and don't let them back in until early evening. Lockouts tend to run from around 10:00 A.M. to 4:00 P.M., during which time your bags might be inside your room—but you won't be.

The practice has its pros and cons. Managers usually justify a lockout by noting that it forces travelers to interact with the locals. The real reason is usually that the hostel can't or won't pay staff to hang around and baby-sit you all day. On the other hand, some hostels become semiresidential situations stuffed with couch potatoes. A lockout sure solves that problem.

In the reviews we've identified those hostels that enforce lockouts. Usually you wouldn't want to be hanging out in the hostel in the middle of the day anyway, but after several sleepless nights of travel—or when you're under the weather—daytime downtime sure is appreciated. So beware.

Some hostels also enforce a maximum limit on your stay—anywhere from three days, if the hostel is really popular, to about two weeks. You will know if such a policy is in effect the moment you walk into a place. If there are lots of cigarette butts, slackers, or dirty clothes hanging around, it's the curse of the dreaded long-termers: folks who came for a day and stay for a lifetime just to avoid finding work. So a maximum-stay rule can be a very good thing. On the other hand, you might find yourself wanting to spend more than three days in some great place—and be shown the door instead.

Savvy budget travelers have learned how to get around this unfortu-
nate situation, of course: They simply suck it up and spend a night at a
convenient motel or B&B—then check back into the cheaper hostel first
thing in the morning. But we didn't tell you to do that. Uh-uh.

etiquette and smarts

Again, to put it simply, use common sense. Hostellers are a refresh-
ingly flexible bunch. All these people are able to make this system
work by looking after one another; remember, in a hostel you're a
community member first and a consumer second. With that in mind,
here are some guidelines for how to act:

- The first thing you should do after check-in is get your bed made.
  When you're assigned a bed, stick to it. Don't spread your stuff
  out on nearby bunks, even if they are empty. Someone's going to
  be coming in late-night for one of them—you can bet the back-
  pack on it.
- Be sure to lock your valuables in a locker or the trunk of your car.
  Good hostels offer lockers as a service; it might cost a little, but
  it's worth it.
- Set toiletries and anything else you need in a place where they
  are easily accessible. This avoids your having to paw through
  your bag late at night, potentially disturbing other guests from
  their slumber. The same goes for early morning departures: If
  you're taking off at the crack of dawn, take precautions not to
  wake the whole place.
- If you're leaving early in the morning, try to make all arrange-
  ments with the manager before going to bed the night before.
  Retrieve your key deposit before the desk closes if possible, and
  settle up any other debts. Managers are usually accommodating
  and pleasant folks, but guests are expected to respect their privacy and peace of mind by not pushing things too far. Dragging a
  manager out of bed at four in the morning to check out—or for
  some other trivial matter—is really pushing it.
- Be sure to mind the bathroom. A quick wiping of the shower floor
  with a paper towel after you use it is common courtesy.
- Finally, be sure to mind the quiet hours. Some hostels have curfews,
  but very few force lights-out. If you are up after hours, be respectful.
  Don't crank the television or radio too loud. (Save that for the
  beach—and for annoying people staying in much nicer digs.)

packing

Those dainty hand towels and dapper shaving kits and free soaps you get at a hotel won't be anywhere in sight at the hostel. In fact, even some of the base essentials may not be available; you're on your own, so bring everything you need to be comfortable.

There are only a few things you can expect the hostel to supply:

- a bed frame with a mattress and pillow
- shower and toilet facilities
- a communal kitchen with pots, pans, and stove
- a common room with some spartan furniture
- maybe a few heavy blankets

Some of the more chic hostels we've identified in this guide may be full-service. Heck, we've stayed in hostels that provide the food for you to cook—not to mention generous spice racks. But they are the exception to the rule.

Bring this stuff to keep your journey through hostel territory comfortable:

- If you're traveling abroad from the United States, you obviously need a passport. Unlike U.S. hostels, an Irish hostel will often take your passport as collateral when you check in. Don't get nervous; this is extremely common. It's the Irish equivalent of taking down your driver's license number when you write a check. However, in the unlikely event that someone loses your passport, make sure you've got backup copies of the issuing office, date, and passport number with you and also back home.
- Hostelling International membership cards are a good thing to have on hand. They can be purchased at many member HI hostels on the road or back home before you go. This card identifies you as a certified superhosteller and gets you the very cheapest rate for your bed in all HI (and also some unaffiliated) hostels. With discounts of $2.00 to $4.00 per night, the savings can add up fast. Cost of membership is $25 for adults ages 18 to 54 and $15 if you're over age 54. Membership is free for kids under age 18.

Sometimes that membership card also gets you deals at local restaurants, bike shops, and tours. Again, it will be easier to deal with the front desk at some of the more cautious hostels (even nonmember ones) if you can flash one of these cards.

- Red Alert! Do not plan on using a sleeping bag in all hostels. A good number of places simply won't allow it—problems with ticks and other creatures dragged in from the great outdoors have propelled this prohibition. The alternative is a sleepsack, which is basically two sheets sewn together with a makeshift pillowcase.

You can find them at most budget travel stores or make your own. Personally we hate these confining wraps, and we rarely get through the night in one without having it twist around our bodies so tight that we wake up wanting to charge it with attempted manslaughter. Our preferred method is to bring our own set of sheets, though that might be too much extra stuff to pack if you're backpacking.

Some hostels give you free linen; most that don't will rent sheets for about $1.00 to $2.00 US per night. You don't get charged for use of the standard army surplus blankets or the musty charm that comes with them.

- Some people bring their own pillows, as those supplied tend to be on the frumpy side. This is a good idea if you're traveling by car and can afford the space.
- We definitely suggest earplugs for light sleepers, especially for urban hostels—but also in case you get caught in a room with a heavy snorer.
- A small flashlight is a must—not only for late-night reading but also to find your bed without waking up the entire dorm.
- A little bit of spice is always nice, especially when you have had one too many plates of pasta. You'll find the cost of basil, oregano, and the like in convenience stores way too high to stomach once you're on the road. Buy it cheap before you leave and pack it in jars or small plastic bags.
- Check which hostels have laundry facilities. It's much easier to do the wash while making dinner than to waste a day sitting around with the cast of The Shining at a local laundromat.
- Wearing flip-flops or other plastic sandals in the shower might help you avoid a dreaded case of athlete's foot.
- Be sure your towel is a quick-drying type. Otherwise you'll wind up with mildew in your pack—and your food.

traveling
in ireland

getting there

FROM NORTH AMERICA BY PLANE

The airline business is crazy: Great deals and rip-off fares come and go with a regularity that is frightening to behold—supply, demand, season, the stock market, and random acts of cruelty or kindness all appear to contribute to the quixotic nature of fares.

As a result, there is no one piece of simple advice we can give you, other than this one: Find a darned good travel agent who cares about budget travelers, and trust him/her with all the planning. You can cruise the Internet if you like, and you might find an occasional great deal your agent doesn't know about. Just make sure the sellers are reputable before giving out that credit-card number.

From the United States, there are direct flights to Ireland on both Irish national carrier Aer Lingus (from such cities as Boston, Chicago, and New York to Dublin and Shannon) and Delta (from Atlanta).

It's also very easy and cheap to connect through London. Fly there first, using any number of airlines; then use the Irish cheapie, Ryanair, from London Stansted to a number of regional airports such as Cork, Knock, and Tralee, in addition to Shannon, Dublin, and Belfast. Special Web-only deals (www.ryanair.ie) sometimes lower the price to as little as €5.00 (about $5.00 US) per direction, but government taxes will also tack at least €20.00 (about $20.00 US) each way onto that figure, so don't get too excited.

Dublin is obviously the biggest hub, the place British Airways, Aer Lingus, American, Canadian, TWA, and other heavyweights use to fly into and out of Ireland; in summer, it can be very tough to get a reasonable fare—or even a seat—unless you book way ahead.

However, Shannon airport (near the River Shannon) is fast becoming popular as a second option. It almost always costs a little more than Dublin if you're coming from North America, but you're rewarded by landing much closer to beautiful western Ireland. If you're planning to bypass Dublin—or save it until the end of your trip—have your travel agent look into Shannon flights. Delta and Aer Lingus fly into Shannon most frequently.

Cork has an airport, too, but it's much smaller and is served only by local flights from Dublin and such.

Cheap-ticket brokers (also called consolidators or bucket shops) are a great bet for saving money, but you have to be fast on your feet to keep up, as the deals appear and disappear literally daily. London and New York are major centers for bucket shops.

FROM EUROPE BY FERRY
The best way to get to Ireland by ferry is probably to take the overnight run from Cherbourg, France, to Cork. Sure, it takes a while, and you have to get out to the Brittany coast. But the reason backpackers like this route is quite simple: The trip is free with a Eurail pass (though you'll pay extra if you want a bed instead of a reclining seat).

FROM ENGLAND BY FERRY
Unless you've flown directly to Ireland, you're probably coming by ferry. From the U.K., you can come via Scotland or Wales by any one of a number of routes; a Eurail or BritRail pass works on a few of them. The companies include the following:

Stena (08705–755755 or 08705–707070) runs two kinds of ferries—regular and high-speed—from Holyhead, Wales, to Dun Laoghaire (a port outside Dublin) and from Fishguard, Wales, to Rosslare in as little as one hour, forty-five minutes. They take cars and bikes, too.

Irish Ferries (0800–0182211) takes you from Holyhead, Wales, right to Dublin in about three hours or from Pembroke, Wales, to Rosslare Harbor (south of Dublin a bit) in under four hours.

P&O Ferries (0870–242–4777) goes from Cairnryan, Scotland, to Larne (just outside Belfast) in one to two hours, with the fare depending on the speed of the ferry you choose.

SeaCat (0345–523–523) ferries you quickly but expensively from Troon, Scotland, or Heysham, England, to Belfast, Northern Ireland, in two and one-half to four hours.

Swansea/Cork Ferries (353–021–4271166) takes travelers from Swansea, Wales, to Cork in ten watery hours.

FROM ENGLAND BY BUS OR TRAIN
Technically, of course, you can't take a bus or train from the U.K. to the Irish mainland. And you probably never will be able to do it via a superlong bridge; the Republic of Ireland enjoys the separation from

England. (Scotland and Northern Ireland nearly touch, though, so you never know. . .)

Nevertheless, it can be done—sort of. If you buy a bus ticket from London to Dublin on a coach, the bus will tote you right onto the ferry. Two that regularly do so are Eurolines (www.eurolines.com) and Bus Eireann (01–83–66111; www.buseireann.ie), Ireland's national bus company.

Trains can't go on these ferries, but they can and do drop travelers off at both the English and Irish docks.

FROM EUROPE BY CAR

It's possible and quite legal to take a French or other Continental car to Ireland by ferry, but we don't recommend it. Why? Simple—the steering wheel's in the wrong place to drive on the other side of the road, which makes corners awfully tricky if someone's passing on the curve. And, shudder to think, people sometimes forget and drive on the wrong side of the road.

FROM ENGLAND BY PLANE

Within Europe, planes used to be fantastically expensive. However, times are changing: A raft of cut-rate short-hop airlines have sprung up recently and can make a trip from England to Ireland incredibly quick and cheap—sometimes much more so than the trains or ferries. The question right now is whether the fierce competition among these upstarts will weed some of them out or not.

From England, British Midland (www.flybmi.com), EasyJet, Ryanair (www.ryanair.com), and Go are the short-hop cheapies of the moment; check for Dublin and Shannon flights. You should be able to go for as little as €30 (about $30 US) round-trip under the right conditions.

FROM NORTHERN IRELAND BY BUS OR TRAIN

It's possible to get from Northern Ireland (which is, of course, part of the United Kingdom) to Ireland pretty easily, too; there'll be security checks, of course, but the transport's good.

By bus, you'd probably take Belfast-based Ulsterbus (028–9033–3000 or 028–9032–011; www.ulsterbus.co.uk) from Belfast or Derry to either Dublin or Donegal. By rail, you take Northern Ireland Railways (028–9066–6630; www.nirailways.co.uk) or Irish Rail (01–836–3333; www.irishrail.ie) from Belfast or Derry, depending on where you're beginning your journey.

getting around ireland

Take a careful look at your transportation options when planning a hostel journey. You should be able to hop from city to city by bus or train without a problem, but you could have trouble getting to rural hostels without a car.

Note that students can get a good deal on Irish transportation by buying a Travelsave Stamp for €10 (about $10 US) from the USIT student travel network or at Ireland's largest transit stations. You've got to be a student or under a certain age, but if you are, this stamp saves you on each long-distance bus or train ride you take while holding it.

BY TRAIN Ireland's national rail company, Irish Rail, is part of the CIE government transport network that helps get you around the country. Call Irish Rail (01–836–3333; www.irishrail.ie) for schedule and fare information. You can generally get anywhere the train serves—which isn't everywhere, unfortunately—for less than €30 (about $30 US) one-way. In the Dublin area, the DART (Dublin Area Rapid Transit) suburban train calls at twenty-five stations within a good-sized radius of the city.

Go whole hog on the Emerald Card to get longer periods of bus and rail access, plus access to Northern Ireland's Ulsterbus and Northern Irish Railways systems. That card costs €170 to € 290 ($170 to $290 US) for eight or fifteen days of riding—half-price if you are under 16—but it's sure worth it if you'll be constantly in motion. Not going far? Buy short-distance tickets one by one at train stations instead.

If you do get some sort of a pass, you've gotta play by the rules: Wait until the first day you're gonna use the pass, then go to the station early and have it validated (stamped) by a ticket agent. Write the current date into the first square (it should have a "1" beneath it)— and remember to put the day first (on top), European-style.

Now it gets easier. Just show your pass to ticket agents when you want to reserve a seat on a train (which is crucial in summer season, on weekends, and during rush hours); that smiling person will hand you a seat reservation, which you show to the conductor. You must reserve seats two hours before the train leaves its first station, and since you'll have no idea where or when that was, it's best to reserve a day or two ahead as you're getting off the train.

Don't fold, bend, or otherwise mangle the long cardboard pass (and that can be difficult to achieve while fumbling for your money belt at the station as the train whips in). That might invalidate the whole thing.

Anyway, the cost of these passes depends on a few things, including how many days you're traveling and how much comfort you want. More days obviously cost more dough. First-class passes, which few hostellers buy, cost 50 percent more and give you a little more legroom. Remember to buy the pass before you get to Ireland.

BY BUS
Buses are cheaper than trains in Ireland, and they go many more places; as a result, you're probably going to spend some time riding them to get anywhere here. (For a trip to, say, Dublin to Cork and back, you'd pay about €20/$20 US, which is roughly half the train fare.) The buses are reasonably on time and scenic, with lots of locals riding alongside you happy to give advice, opinions, or soccer scores. You might have to wait around for one, but eventually there'll be a bus going wherever you're going; just remember that on Sundays and certain Mondays, some lines run less frequently.

Irish Bus is the country's national bus carrier (also known by its Galeic name, Bus Eireann). Call the headquarters in Dublin (01–83–66111) for rates, schedules, bus station information, and other stuff. Or peruse their comprehensive Web site—www.buseireann.ie—for schedule and rate details.

Local buses fill the rest of the gaps, and these can range from incredibly efficient lines to laughable ones.

BY CAR
Renting a car is definitely a more expensive way to see Ireland, and yet it has advantages: You can cover the hamlets a whole lot quicker, you have complete freedom of movement, and you get that cool feeling of the wind and rain rushing past your ears if you've forgotten to roll up the window.

Just bring your wallet: Rentals in Ireland go for a good $60 US a day, and that might or might not include heavy taxes and insurance. Rent or lease long-term through a company like Kemwel (1–800–678–0678; www.kemwel.com), which does short- and long-term rentals for a fraction of the normal European daily rate if you book ahead from your home country. AutoEurope (1–800–223–5555) is a related service. If you make a last-minute decision (nah, not you) to do it while in Ireland, the Dan Dooley firm (1–800–331–9301 from the US, 062–53103 from Ireland, and 0800–282189 from the UK) is a local source. Some of the North American biggies are also easily found at airports and train stations.

You won't use as much gas as in the United States because it's a smaller car, but it'll cost—more than $5.00 a gallon at last check. (Want a bike yet?) Gas is measured in liters, and there are roughly four liters to the U.S. gallon. Gas prices are listed per liter, so multiply by four and then convert into home currency to estimate the price per gallon you'd pay back home.

If you're still going to rent, remember this cardinal rule. YOU GOTTA DRIVE ON THE LEFT. Sound simple? Not exactly. Our tip? Keep your body in the middle of the road. The other tricky part is shifting with your left hand instead of your right, while your feet continue to do the same clutch-gas dance they do on an American car. It's a bit like learning a new hokey-pokey—clumsy as heck at first, and you don't want to make a mistake with a busload of tourists screaming toward you at 60 miles an hour. So practice in a parking lot first.

Next issue: numbers. Confusingly, speeds and distances in Ireland are measured both in miles and kilometers, depending apparently on local custom—and miles actually seem to be winning the battle. Make sure you know which one's being used on your road sign, map, or speed limit sign.

Just to remind you: 1 mile is about 1⁶⁄₁₀ kilometers; 100 miles is roughly 160 kilometers. Here are some common speed limits you might see on road signs, with their U.S. equivalents:

40 kph = 25 miles per hour
100 kph = 62 miles per hour
50 kilometers away = 31 miles away

Basically, to convert miles to kilometers, multiply by 1.6. To convert kilometers to miles, multiply by .6.

Stop signs are rare, but when present they're round and red. More often, you'll slow down at a dotted line, then merge with traffic.

BY BIKE Bicycle is one of the very best ways of all to see Ireland; though challenging at times, the terrain rewards cyclists with view after splendiferous view.

Rental agencies are everywhere—and many hostels within this book rent two-wheelers out, as well—or you could try one of the many tour outfitters that run country-road tours of various regions.

The national clearinghouse for cycling information and tours is in Dublin. Contact Walking Cycling Ireland (P.O. Box 5520, Ballsbridge, Dublin 4) at 01–668–8278.

BY MINIBUS The most popular kind of backpacker travel these days is swiftly becoming the "JOJO" (jump on, jump off) minibus services that circle the country like sharks, scooping up backpackers in far-away train stations and depositing them safely in remote, beautiful places. It's also known as HOHO, which is hop-on and hop-off. (Whatever.)

Inevitably, Ireland has also developed its own homegrown JOJO/HOHO bus services much as Scotland, England, Wales, and Northern Ireland have done.

Irish Rover Tours (01–836–4684; www.tirnanogtours.com) runs three- and six-day circular tours of the Emerald Isle that cost anywhere from €90 to €170 (about $90 to $170 US). As a bonus to hostellers, their morning starting points are always at a string of Dublin hostels.

money

In 2002 the euro became the official currency of most countries in Western Europe (with the notable exception of the United Kingdom), replacing the hallowed Irish punt. Though it's much more brightly colored and designed than American bills, this isn't play money.

The notes—that's what they call paper money over there, not "bills"—come in denominations of blue 5s, pinkish 10s, sky-blue 20s, orangey 50s, mean green 100s, yellow-bellied 200s (yes, 200s), and purple-hazy 500s. Euro coins (in other words, the change) are roughly similar to Canadian and American coinage. There's a 1 cent coin, a unique 2 cent coin, a 5 cent coin, a 10 cent coin, a 20 cent coin, a 50 cent coin, a one dollar coin with a gold rim and a silver center, and a two dollar coin with a silver rim around a gold center.

Remember that a euro is worth, very roughly, one U.S. dollar; the actual value fluctuates widely, depending on exchange rates. When the euros first appeared they were worth a bit less than a buck a pop; at press time, however, their value was more like $1.10 each.

In Northern Ireland you'll get a slightly different kind of cash from the ATM or the change bureau: They're actually British pounds sterling (known simply as pounds), but they look a little different because they're printed by banks in Northern Ireland. They're worth exactly the same as pounds in England. Don't expect to use your euros here, except in border towns, where the merchants might accept them.

If you're going to Wales or England afterward, note that you can't spend your Northern Ireland–printed pounds there, so change them before you leave, if possible. (You can use British or even Scottish pound notes in Northern Ireland with no trouble at all, however.)

phones

Using Irish phones isn't much different from using British phones.

All phone and fax numbers in this book are listed as though dialed from within Ireland or from within Northern Ireland. So when you're in either country, dial the numbers exactly as listed in the interior of this book and be sure to include the first zero. That zero is required for calling long distance within each country.

To call from outside these countries, you'll need to add prefixes.

To call Ireland from the United States, first dial 011–353 and then dial the number as printed inside the book—but drop the first zero from the number as listed or the call won't go through.

To call Ireland from other European countries (and that includes from Britain and Northern Ireland), dial 00–353 before all the phone numbers in this book, then drop the first zero from the phone number as listed inside the book or the call won't go through.

To call Northern Ireland from the United States, dial 011–44, then drop the first zero from the number listed in the interior of the book.

To call Northern Ireland from Ireland, dial 08, then dial the number exactly as listed in the book, making sure to include the first zero. Note: Many Northern Ireland phone numbers have undergone a recent change. We have made every effort to correct numbers, but please check to make sure the number is right by calling information.

Pay phones take coins or cards, but cards are infinitely easier and are becoming increasingly popular. Otherwise, you'll have to keep feeding coins into the slot—or get cut off in mid-sentence.

speaking irish

Irish English isn't exactly the same thing as American English, and it's not even exactly the same as British English either. But you'll get the hang of it once you decipher the gorgeous Irish accent on things. And many of the terms are pretty much the same as they'd be in England, except with slight twists in pronunciation or meaning.

Hereforth, a very brief primer on some of the key Irish-English words you'll need to know:

SPEAKING IRISH . . .

What they say	How they say it (approximately)	What they mean
craic	crack	fun, camaraderie
pint	paint	glass of beer
pissed	pist	drunk
loo	Lou	bathroom, toilet
trad	trad	Irish folk music
snog	snog	kiss
slag	slag	make fun of
lough	lock	lake
queue	Q	a line
mind	mined	be careful of
flat	flat	apartment
flatmate	flat mate	roommate
coach	coach	intercity bus
lorry	Laurie	truck

. . . AND GAELIC

Since Ireland is officially bilingual, Gaelic is still prevalent in pockets of rural areas in the north and west. This will sound like complete gibberish to the uninitiated—oh, you might think it's German for a second when you hear it on the bus, but it's not. Gaelic has its own vocabulary, rules of grammar, spellings, and pronunciations; it can be mastered, but not here and not quickly.

Your best bet? Take a class; they're available around the country, especially in the gaeltachts (official Gaelic-speaking heritage areas) or at universities.

All right, here's just a bit of Gaelic for you, too:

SPEAKING GAELIC

What they say	How they say it (approximately)	What they mean
dia dhuit	Chia ditch	hi there
dia's muire dhuit	Chias my word! ditch	hi, yourself
failte	fault Shah	welcome
An Lahr	on-lar	downtown
tra	th'raw	the beach
ceilidh	Kay Lee	Irish folk dance
fir	fear	guys
mna	minnaw	gals
slainte	slahnzhe	cheers! bottoms up!

other
resources

Two of three main hostel organizations are based in Dublin, and, while all three groups possess quite different personalities, each is pretty efficient and helpful about getting you the goods on its respective members' hostels. Telephone numbers are listed here as if calling from North America.

An Oige (Irish Youth Hostel Association)
61 Mountjoy Street
Dublin 7
Ireland
Telephone: +011–353–(0)1–830–4555
Fax: +011–353–(0)1–830–5808
E-mail: mailbox@anoige.ie
Web site: www.irelandyha.org

Independent Holiday Hostels of Ireland (IHH)
57 Lower Gardiner Street
Dublin 1
Ireland
Telephone: +011–353–(0)1–836–4700
Fax: +011–353–(0)1–836–4710
E-mail: ihh@iol.ie
Web site: www.hostels-ireland.com

Independent Hostels Owners Ireland (IHO)
c/o Dooey Hostel
Glencolmcille, Donegal
Ireland
Telephone: +011–353–(0)73–30130
Fax: +011–353–(0)73–30339
Web site: www.holidaybound.com/ihi/

We've added Northern Ireland hostels to the end of this book, since many hostellers traveling in Ireland end up there as well. The following group is associated with Hostelling International.

Hostelling International Northern Ireland (HINI)
22 Donegall Road
Belfast BT12 5JN
Northern Ireland
Telephone: +011–44–(0)1232–324733
Fax: +011–44–(0)1232–439699
Web site: www.hini.org.uk

The best place to get information about Ireland is from its fairly efficient tourist offices; though all of them seem friendly enough, they tend to load you down with a few too many glossy brochures depicting places you'll never get to. Funny how the sun's always shining in those pics, too.

Anyway, these folks are sensitive to the needs of backpackers—a nice switch from the North American way of doing things. Just forgive them for occasionally trying to stick you in an expensive B&B instead of directing you to a hostel they've "never heard of."

Haven't got time to deal with the tourist offices? Hit the Web running then, starting somewhere around here:

www.hostels-ireland.com

The IHH independent hostel chain has its Web page here, a synopsis of its hostels plus contact information.

www.ireland.travel.ie
www.tourismIreland.com

These are the official tourism sites for the Irish Republic, containing good basics on the place.

Here are a few additional Web sites that will be useful:

Dublin: www.visitdublin.com
www.southeastireland.travel.ie
East and Southeast Ireland: www.midlandseastireland.travel.ie
Northern Ireland: www.discovernorthernireland.com
Hostelling International Northern Ireland: www.hini.org.uk
An Oige, the Irish Youth Hostel Association: www.irelandyha.org

final advice

There's surprisingly little out there about hostelling and hostels (that's why you're reading this, right?) but we did find a few sources. Most simply list phone numbers and addresses.

Just remember that we've done our best, but hostels are constantly opening, closing, renovating, being sold, and changing their policies. So not everything written in a guidebook will always still be true by the time you read it. Be smart and call ahead to confirm prices, availability, and directions, rather than rolling into town depending on a bed—and getting a nasty surprise like a vacant lot instead. We know; it has happened to us.

Good luck!

the
hostels

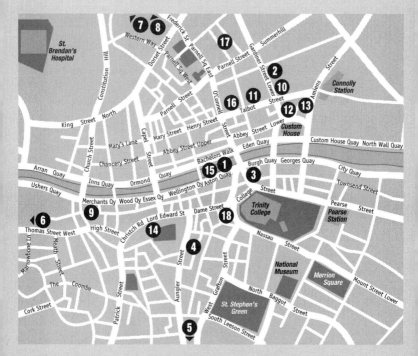

dublin

This is probably why you've come to Ireland: to experience Dublin in all its hectic glory—the bookshops, rain, pubs, pictures of U2 and James Joyce plastered around town . . . and much, much more. After weeks running around the Irish countryside, coming here can be a bit overwhelming—but it's sure to inject a bit of cosmopolitan culture in any trip that has started to degenerate into a string of rainy days or dull meals.

Getting around Dublin isn't too hard at all. The central city is very compact, based along both sides of the River Liffey, so much of it's walkable. Buses run seemingly everywhere else you want to go, too; Dublin Bus (01–873-4222) offers everything from one-day to one-month passes on its extensive network of services in both the urban and suburban areas. You can buy tickets from drivers, at more than 200 offices in the greater Dublin region, at the central O'Connell Street Station, or at still another office at Dublin Airport. (Bear in mind that not all bus drivers are able to give change.)

If you'll be using only buses while in town, get the Dublin Rambler pass. You can travel for three hassle-free days around town on the Dublin Bus (Bus Eireann) system and also use the Airlink service to and from the airport.

You can reach some hostels just outside the city using the DART suburban trains that chug north and south from the city center to such quaint-sounding places as Howth and Dun Laoghaire. The city's municipal transit system sells various passes for frequent train or train and bus users; an all-inclusive one will run about €4.50 (about $5.00 US) per day or €16.50 (about $17.00 US) for a week. It's valid on almost everything except the city's special night buses.

Once safely in the city, hostels are amazingly thick on the ground here—and most of them are darned good. Call the independent, IHH-affiliated joints first; though laid-back, they offer the best mixture of socializing and comfy beds.

Around town, besides the obvious Big Three draws—St. Stephen's Green, Trinity College, and the hip Temple Bar neighborhood—there are an amazing number of other old castles, buildings, and parks scattered within the city limits. Dublin Castle is the most central, but there's also Rathfarnham Castle (built in 1583 and pretty impressive), the National Botanic Gardens (more than 20,000 species of things growing here), the Pearse Museum, and the spooky Kilmainham Gaol.

All have small admission charges and daytime open hours, and they can be reached by public buses.

Just north of the city, the Lusk Heritage Centre doles out history in a cool setting—a rounded tower built in the 800s (yes, the 800s) plus an old belfry and a "newer" church built in the 1800s. You can reach it by taking the 33 bus. The Bru na Boinne Centre, another historic building, is the jumping-off point if you want to visit megalithic (stone, that is) tombs.

For a quickie introduction to some of Dublin's key sights, your best bet might be to get the city's SuperSaver Card—a one-day pass that, despite the lame name, gets you into the Joyce Museum, the castle at Malahide, and a bunch of other attractions.

At night? Well, what else? We love to hit the pubs, of course; you can't walk 10 feet without stumbling into another one. O'Shea's Merchant on Bridge Street is typical: The walls are plastered with photos and old knicknacks that give a real sense of continuity and history to the place. Locals file in to play the real Irish music, not the stuff you get on package tours. There's a tinge of sadness—always the sadness—but a sense, too, that people come here to acknowledge life.

That's the best of Dublin: life pressing forward in defiant, even jubilant, celebration. Think U2. Now you're getting the picture.

dublin hostels
at a glance

HOSTEL	RATING	COST	IN A WORD	PAGE
Globetrotters	◪	€15–€25	fancy	45
Marlborough	◪	€11.50–€19	clean	51
Kinlay House	◪	€15–€18	central	49
Four Courts	◪	€15–€27	new	44
Litton Lane	◪	€15–€25	historic	50
Jacob's Inn Hostel	◪	€13–€23	comfy	48
Ashfield House	◪	€13–€34	good	37
Belgrave Hall	◪	€12–€15	handsome	40
Brewery Hostel	◪	€18–€36	cheery	41
Abbey Court		€18–€26	friendly	36
Avalon House		€15–€20	tight	38
Celts House		€11–€19	homey	42
Dublin Int'l		€20	institutional	43
Isaac's Hostel		€11–€18	noisy	47
Gogarty's Hostel		€15–€30	happy	53
Goin' My Way Hostel		€13	tall	47
Mount Eccles Court Hostel		€13–€30	decent	52
Abraham House		€13–€34	worn	36

abbey court hostel

29 Bachelor's Walk, O'Connell Bridge, Dublin

Phone Number: 01–878–0700
Fax: 01–878–0719
E-mail: info@abbey-court.com
Rates: €18–€26 per person (about $18–$26 US), doubles €76–€88 (about $76–$88 US)
Credit cards: Yes
Beds: 228
Private/family rooms: Yes
Extras: Meals, Internet access ($), Laundry

You can't get any closer to the famous O'Connell Bridge than this hostel; it's practically right on top of the thing.

Gestalt: Abbey Road
Party Index:

They've got dorms, family rooms, Internet access for a fee, and laundry— and they serve meals, too. You're just across the river from the hip Temple Bar area, where everybody wants to be, and Trinity College.

how to get there:

By bus: From Busarus station, walk ¼ mile along Abbey Street or along river to O'Connell Bridge; hostel is just past bridge, on right.
By car: Contact hostel for directions.
By train: From Connelly Station, walk 300 yards to river, turn right, and continue about ⅓ mile to O'Connell Bridge. Hostel is just past bridge, on right.

abraham house hostel

82-83 Lower Gardiner Street, Dublin 1

Phone Number: 01–855–0600
Fax: 01–855–0598
E-mail: stay@abraham-house.ie
Rates: €13–€34 per person ($13–$34 US)
Credit cards: Yes
Beds: 191
Private/family rooms: Yes
Kitchen available: Yes
Office hours: Twenty-four hours

Affiliation: IHH
Extras: Bureau de change, breakfast, laundry, TV, pool table, restaurant ($),
Internet, towels

Not exactly central, this place might be a good bet if you're getting in
late or getting out early—it's on the way to Dublin's out-of-town airport.

Dorms come in rooms of four to ten beds, and they also do private
rooms. They change currency, serve a breakfast, and maintain the
usual TV room and pool table combo.
Overall, the place is just so-so—possibly from heavy use, as it's always
been a very popular place for some
reason. (Take note and book ahead if
you're really set on staying here.)

Staff and management do a pretty
good job here of making you feel at

Gestalt:
Abraham sandwich
Hospitality:
Cleanliness:
Party index:

home. It's just that the facilities aren't Dublin's tops; complaints
include worn plumbing, a skimpy breakfast, and other quibbles. That's
the price of popularity. Getting one of the twenty private rooms could
improve the experience, though.

Let's just say that it's in the middle of the Dublin pack: unspectac-
ular and showing wear and tear, but certainly not the pits. That distant
location, though, makes it an unlikely pick.

how to get there:

By bus: Bus station in Dublin; call hostel for transit route.
By car: Call hostel for directions.
By train: Train station in Dublin; call hostel for transit route.

ashfield house

19-20 D'Olier Street, Dublin 2

Phone Number: 01–679–7734
Fax: 01–679–0852
E-mail: ashfield@indigo.ie
Rates: €13–€34 per person (about $13–$34 US); doubles €30–€46 (about
$30–$46 US)
Credit cards: Yes

Beds: 104
Private/family rooms: Yes
Kitchen available: Yes
Office hours: Twenty-four hours
Affiliation: IHH
Extras: Breakfast, meals ($), laundry, bike rentals, bureau de change, laundry, cafe

How'd they do that? It's a Dublin hostel with really excellent position near that awesome Temple Bar area we keep telling you so much about. (Watch for U2 sightings, just in case our favorite stood-the-test-of-time band decides to show up at a pub near the hostel steps for a beer.)

Gestalt: Ashfield of dreams
Hospitality: 🏨
Cleanliness: 🏨
Party index: 🎉🎉🎉

Oh, the hostel. Right. It's certainly fine—good enough to get the nod from our hosteller scouts as one of the top tier in Dublin. Put that together with the busy but cool setting, and you've got near-perfect hostelling forecast.

The dorms at Ashfield contain the usual number of beds—in this case, usually four to twelve apiece—and they are more pleasant than we have any right to expect them to be. They even throw in a kitchen for fixing meals, bureau de change, free breakfast, laundry service (that costs money), and a cafe if you're feeling lazy.

The staff will rent you a bike, too, although we'd recommend seeing this hustle-bustle town on foot.

how to get there:

By bus: Call hostel for transit route.
By car: Call hostel for directions.
By train: Call hostel for transit route.

avalon house

55 Aungier Street, Dublin 2

Phone Number: 01–475–0001
Fax: 01–475–0303
E-mail: info@avalon-house.ie

Rates: €15–€20 per person (about $15–$20 US); doubles €56–€74 (about $56–$74 US)
Credit cards: Yes
Beds: 281
Private/family rooms: Yes
Kitchen available: No
Office hours: Twenty-four hours
Affiliation: IHH
Extras: Cafe ($), bureau de change, breakfast, laundry, TV, fireplace, lockers, Internet

We'd like to give our highest marks to Avalon House, universally checked off by our hostellers as one of Dublin's better hostels. We'd like to, but we can't; it wants to be home away from home, but it too often turns out to be more like a warehouse.

A brick building that once housed a medical school, it's quite close to wonderful Trinity College, St. Stephen's Green, and the hub of Dublin. (Would that make it Hublin?) Everything's run smoothly and interestingly by likable staff.

The entire first floor at Avalon is a cafe with cheap, delicious food. This restaurant and coffee shop are two good bets in the city's sometimes bleak eating scene. Dorms here, in a separate area, generally contain four to ten beds, and they're okay—but can get quite crowded and loud, as they're just too small to handle the load. Some have en-suite bathrooms, which is good, but they're not as sweet and clean as they could be.

Gestalt: Halfalon
Safety:
Hospitality:
Party index:

At least you can book one of the private rooms, change money, hang with fellow hostellers in the common area, and get accustomed to the coed hall bathrooms.

Oh, and one more big bonus if you're starting your Irish sojourn here: Stay a night and you can book all your future IHH nights from here to save the hassle of doing it later.

how to get there:

By bus: Call hostel for transit route.
By car: Call hostel for directions.
By ferry: Take 46A bus to downtown.
By train: From DART, take train to Pearse Station.

key to icons

Attractive natural setting	Comfortable beds	Good for active travelers
Ecologically aware hostel	A particularly good value	Visual arts at hostel or nearby
Superior kitchen facilities or cafe	Wheelchair accessible	Music at hostel or nearby
Offbeat or eccentric place	Good for business travelers	Great hostel for skiers
Superior bathroom facilities	Especially well suited for families	Bar or pub at hostel or nearby
Romantic private rooms		Editors' choice: among our very favorite hostels

belgrave hall hostel

34 Belgrave Square, Monkstown (Dublin)

Phone Number: 01–284–2106
Fax: 01–280–5838
E-mail: info@dublinhostel.com
Rates: €12–€15 per person (about $12–$15 US)
Credit cards: Yes
Beds: 50
Private/family rooms: Yes
Kitchen available: Yes
Affiliation: IHH, IHO
Extras: Breakfast, bike rentals, laundry, car rentals, meals ($), Internet access, fireplace

Situated not in Dublin but a bit south of it, Belgrave Hall is pretty nicely outfitted and quite close to the Stena ferry dock in Dun Laoghaire if that town's hostel is already full up. It's better than most, thanks to a good facility with equally good management.

The early-Victorian building was constructed in 1840 and once served as the summer home of the Bishop of Meath (that's a county). Today, the high-ceilinged dorm rooms contain from two to six comfortable beds each, and every room comes with a small en-suite bathroom tucked into it. The owner has added or refurbished some nice touches—wood floors, carpets, marble mantelpieces, friezes, atmospheric old chairs, dressers, detail on the ceilings, and such—that almost make the place a history lesson in itself.

Party index:

But that's not all. They've also added modern services, including Internet and e-mail access, open turf fires, and bike and car rentals. The common room here is especially nice, featuring computer with said access as well as a comfy new couch in front of a roaring fire, a writing table, and a chess board.

Ah, we didn't even mention the hostel's position right on Dublin Bay. Great views abound. As one more tremendous bonus, the Irish Cultural Institute is literally next door; you need walk no more than a few steps from the hostel door to catch all that traditional folk music you came here to hear.

To get here, you take the DART train south of the city between Blackrock and Monkstown.

how to get there:

By bus: From Dublin bus station, walk to Tara Street DART station; take DART train south to Seapoint Station. Walk down Seapoint Avenue to Belgrave Road, turn right, then turn left onto Belgrave Square. Go clockwise around square to number 34.

By car: From Dublin, take M50 ring road to N81 exit; exit and follow Stena Ferry signs to Blackrock, then take Seapoint Avenue to Belgrave Road. Turn left on Belgrave, then left onto Belgrave Square.

By train: From Dublin, take DART train south to Seapoint Station. Walk down Seapoint Avenue to Belgrave Road, turn right, then turn left onto Belgrave Square. Go clockwise around square to number 34.

brewery hostel

22-23 Thomas Street, Dublin 8

Phone Number: 01–453–8600
Fax: 01–453–8616
E-mail: breweryh@indigo.ie
Rates: €18–€36 per person (about $18–$36 US); doubles €65–€80 (about $65–$80 US)

Credit cards: Yes
Beds: 52
Private/family rooms: Yes
Kitchen available: Yes
Office hours: Twenty-four hours
Affiliation: IHH
Extras: Breakfast, pickups, TV, VCR, grill, terrace, laundry, fax, lockers

Once you get here you'll see why it's called the Brewery Hostel. Grand old Guinness is only steps away, and chances are good that you'll

Gestalt: Beer with us
Hospitality:
Cleanliness:
Safety:
Party index:

spend half a day in there checking out the brewing of the black beverage that's almost a religion in Ireland.

This place, like most IHH joints, is as relaxed as you'd want it to be. Maybe too much so—dorms tend to be mixed-sex, which some hostellers loved and others despised. But the rooms are spacious, airy, and cheery, with newish bunks. They contain four, eight, or ten beds each, all with en-suite bathrooms, and they maintain some double rooms for couples, too.

Breakfast is free, and they've added lots of social amenities like a TV room and common area with comfy couches, plus—in the warm season—an outdoor patio with a grill. Some love it, some merely like it, but most agree it's very good.

how to get there:

By bus: From O'Connell or Dame Street, take 123 bus to hostel.
By car: Call hostel for directions.
By train: From Heuston Station, walk up Steevens Lane and turn immediately left onto Thomas Street. Hostel is across street, just past Guinness brewery.

celts house hostel

32 Blessington Street, Dublin 7

Phone Number: 01–830–0657
Fax: 01–830–0479

E-mail: res@celtshouse.iol.ie
Rates: €11–€19 per person (about $11–$19 US); doubles €20–€34(about $20–$34 US)
Credit cards: Yes
Beds: 38
Private/family rooms: Yes
Affiliation: IHH
Extras: Meals ($), bike rentals, Internet, sheets ($)

The IHH just keeps crankin'—this time with a small Irish-named place that's been the focus of some recent renovation work, by the look of it. Not a complete party-animal place, it's instead one of the town's more homey joints.

Party index:

how to get there:

By bus: Call hostel for transit route.
By car: Call hostel for directions.
By train: Call hostel for transit route.

dublin international hostel

61 Mountjoy Street, Dublin 7

Phone Number: 01–830–1766
Fax: 01–830–1600
Rates: €20 per HI member (about $20 US); doubles €50–€56 (about $50–$56 US)
Credit cards: Yes
Beds: 369
Private/family rooms: 14
Kitchen available: Yes
Office hours: Twenty-four hours
Affiliation: HI-AO
Extras: Breakfast, meals ($), laundry, conference room, bureau de change, tours, Internet access, bike rentals, parking, TV, shuttle service, luggage storage ($), sheets ($)

A former convent packed with anywhere from 350 to 540 beds (depends on whom you ask on which day), this place is huge and uninspiring. At first glance it's got all the charm of a nun's whack on the knuckles with a ruler, and it's not in the greatest neighborhood, either—a bit of a sketchy area up on the workabout north side of the city. So don't go walking around outside alone at night if you can help it; the security precautions aren't supertight.

Gestalt: Nun of the above

Hospitality:

Cleanliness:

Party index:

So why'd we stay? We had to. Naw, just kiddin'. Actually, it's halfway decent, although that institutional taste never quite goes away.

Dorms are pretty bleak—packed, big, with basic beds that are sometimes comfy and sometimes uncomfy—but the cafe and kitchen partially redeem the place. Also, some rooms have their own bathrooms, so you don't always have to fumble your way to distant loos at 3:00 A.M. There are fewer rules here than in many An Oige–affiliated joints, too, and it's kept obsessively clean.

They also kick in plenty of services like decent food, free big breakfasts, and a currency exchange. So it's not completely terrible or anything, just kinda sterile.

Our advice: If you're still coming, come early and pay extra for a two-to-six-bedded dorm. And watch out for the ghost of Sister Mary, wielding a ruler she'll take to uncouth hostellers. Just kiddin'—again.

how to get there:

By bus: From downtown, take 10 bus 1 mile to hostel.

By ferry: Ferry from Holyhead, Wales, to Dublin dock (2½ miles away), then catch Stena bus to Central Station, 1 mile from hostel. From Dun Laoghire (7½ miles), catch Stena bus to Central Station.

By foot: From O'Connell Street bridge, drive north to Parnell Street; make a left, then right on Parnell Square. Go 4 blocks to Mountjoy.

By plane: From airport, take 41A bus to near hostel.

By train: Connolly Station is 1 mile; Heuston Station is 2 miles.

four courts hostel

15–17 Merchants Quay, Dublin 8

Phone Number: 01–672–5839
Fax: 01–672–5862

E-Mail: info@fourcourtshostel.com
Web site: www.fourcourtshostel.com
Rates: €15–€27 per person (about $15–$27 US); doubles €55–€66 (about $55–$66 US)
Credit cards: Yes
Beds: 230
Private/family rooms: Yes
Kitchen available: Yes
Office hours: 24 hours
Affiliation: None
Extras: Internet access, laundry, bureau de change, lounge, game room, pool tables, tour desk, breakfast

This huge, newish independent hostel has a riverside location (right on the Liffey), and though it's a little bit of a hike to Trinity, Grafton Street, and everything else you wanna see, this place delivers on amenities, friendliness, modernity, and cleanliness. In short, it's a very good base hostel for exploring the city is you don't mind wearing out a little shoe leather.

Gestalt:
Courts and spark
Hospitality:
Cleanliness:
Party Index:

It's made up of three connected Georgian mansions, fitted out with dorms containing anywhere from four to ten beds apiece. There is also a selection of double rooms for couples and families. Laundry? Parking? Front desk security? Big screen TVs? Kitchen? Free continental breakfast? Natch. There's even an elevator, for crying out loud.

how to get there:

By bus: From Busarus station, take 90 bus to hostel
By car: Contact hostel for directions.
By ferry: Take 53 or 53A bus to city center
By train: From Heuston or Connolly Station, take 90 bus to hostel.
By plane: From Dublin airport, take 748 bus to hostel.

globetrotters tourist hostel

46-48 Lower Gardiner Street, Dublin 1

Phone Number: 01–873–5893
Fax: 01–878–8787

E-mail: gtrotter@indigo.ie
Rates: €15–€25 per person (about $15–$25 US); doubles €60–€120 (about $60–$120 US)
Credit cards: Yes
Beds: 250
Office hours: Twenty-four hours
Affiliation: IHH
Extras: Breakfast, meals, laundry, sheets, luggage storage, TV, Internet

You're not always going to get it this good.

We were amazed at the Globetrotters, which (we've gotta admit) is a word we've seen hostels around the world slap onto their front doors—often with dire conse-

Gestalt:
World party
Hospitality:
Cleanliness:
Safety:
Party index:

quences. Memo to managers: Just calling yerself a globetrotter doesn't mean you've accomplished it. Too often, it's the bedbugs doing the trotting.

Anyhow, this dapper place scored big right off the bat with a delicious and filling breakfast buffet that's included with your bed price—and get this: It's AYCE. That's right, All You Can Eat. Some hostellers wedged themselves out the front door hours later.

Then we discovered the nifty courtyard garden, another nicety.

Granted, some of the dorms are ten-bed affairs, and the doubles cost more. But if you've snagged one of the thirty-eight private B&B–style rooms, you know this is pretty cool anyway: B&B, plus hostel-ling companions, all in one shot. Even the dorms are relatively comfy.

What else can we say? Oh, how about this: This palatial hostel is just a block from Dublin's main bus station, maybe 2 blocks from its train station, and the neighborhood actually doesn't suffer too badly. Just in case, though, security here is tight.

how to get there:

By bus: From bus station, walk 1 block to hostel.
By car: Call hostel for directions.
By train: From train station, walk 2 blocks to hostel.

goin' my way hostel

Cardijn House, 15 Talbot Street, Dublin 1

Phone Number: 01–878–8484 or 01–878–8618
Fax: 01–878–8091
Rates: €13 per person (about $13 US); doubles €40 (about $40 US)
Beds: 40
Private/family rooms: Yes
Season: April 1 to December 22
Affiliation: IHH
Extras: Breakfast, coffee shop, meals ($)
Lockout: 10:00 A.M. to 5:00 P.M.
Curfew: Midnight

Hard to find and not so wonderful that you'll want to stay for years, this hostel even changes its name periodically. And it's the only hostel in Dublin that charges you for showers, locks you out, and has a nighttime curfew.

Gestalt: Goin' away

Party index: 🎉🎉🎉

In general, it's an average joint—made less likable by the knee-straining hike to the sixth floor you might have to make if you've drawn one of those rooms. Things are simple and too tightly packed (there are usually six to eight beds per tiny room), so it's definitely not a first-choice pick when in Dublin.

Only benefit? A semi-interesting Dublinesque location on a regular street above those all-knowing cogs of Irish life, the news agents.

how to get there:

By bus: Call hostel for transit route.
By car: Call hostel for directions.
By train: Call hostel for transit route.

isaac's dublin hostel

2-5 Frenchmans Lane, Dublin 1

Phone Number: 01–855–6215
Fax: 01–855–6574
E-mail: hostel@isaacs.ie
Rates: €11–€18 per person (about $11–$18 US); doubles €52–€66 (about $52–$66 US)

Credit cards: Yes
Beds: 235
Private/family rooms: Yes
Office hours: Twenty-four hours
Affiliation: IHH
Extras: Cafe ($), bike rentals, lockers, bureau de change, music, meals ($)
Lockout: 11:00 A.M. to 5:00 P.M.

This eighteenth-century building was once a warehouse for a wine merchant. Now it's a rockin' hostel, professionally run and almost legendary among the droves of hostellers who descend on Dublin each summer.

The place, despite its hugeness, is very good: singles, big but still fun dorms, lots of private rooms, decent food, some bathrooms right in the rooms, and even regular live-music nights to inititate you into the Irish way as soon as you've arrived.

However—and it's a big however—this place definitely isn't for light sleepers. You couldn't sleep any closer to the train tracks if you wanted to (not that you do): They literally run right over the place. (Actually, it reminded us of the scene in The Blues Brothers where Jake and Elwood Blues nap in Elwood's apartment, right underneath Chicago's elevated train.)

Gestalt: Train a comin'
Hospitality:
Party index:

Also, there's an annoying six-hour lockout during the heart of the day, and the place isn't the supercleanest.

how to get there:

By bus: From Busarus bus station, walk around corner to hostel.
By car: Call hostel for directions.
By train: Take DART to Connolly Station, then walk along Talbot Street to Frenchmans Lane and turn left to hostel.

jacob's inn hostel

21–28 Talbot Place, Dublin 1

Phone Number: 01–855–5660
Fax: 01–855–5664

E-mail: jacobs@issacs.ie
Rates: €13–€23 per person (about $13–$23 US); doubles €60–€76 (about $60–$76 US)
Credit cards: Yes
Beds: 295
Private/family rooms: Yes
Office hours: Twenty-four hours
Affiliation: IHH
Extras: Meals ($), TV, pool table, bureau de change, laundry
Lockout: 11:00 A.M. to 3:00 P.M.

Incredibly close to Dublin's main bus station and pretty good overall, this biggish hostel somehow still manages to be friendly. It sports good-sized dorm rooms—with around six beds apiece, usually—but also a

Gestalt: Jacob's ladder
Hospitality:
Party Index:

good supply of doubles, triples, and quads for couples and families.

Plus there are other amenities, like a little restaurant that stays open all day long, good en-suite bathrooms in the dorms, a currency exchange, a television room, and more. We liked the key-card system of getting in, too.

how to get there:

By bus: Near Busarus bus station.
By car: Call hostel for directions.
By train: Take DART to Connolly Station, then walk along Talbot Street to Talbot Place; turn left to hostel.

kinlay house hostel
2-12 Lord Edward Street, Dublin 2

Phone Number: 01–679–6644
Fax: 01–679–7437
E-mail: kinlay.dublin@usit.ie
Rates: €15–€18 per person (about $15–$18 US); doubles €50–€66 (about $50–$66 US)
Credit Cards: Yes
Beds: 149
Private/family rooms: Yes
Office hours: Twenty-four hours

Affiliation: IHH
Extras: Breakfast, cafe ($), laundry, bike rentals, bureau de change, lockers, TV

This is it: the southern Dublin Temple Bar neighborhood you've heard so much about—and Irish rock stars.

And Kinlay House's brick Victorian supplies some of the best-positioned, if not the most comfortable, bunks in town. Beds come packed four to six to a room, usually, unless you grab one of a dozen or so private rooms (some with en-suite bathrooms, thank goodness).

Gestalt: Kin-do
Hospitality:
Cleanliness:
Party index:

It's a nice building, run by the youth tourist group USIT, with great views of town. You'll like the laid-back atmosphere, the laundry, and the continental breakfast they throw in with your bed price. You might love or hate the mostly coed nature of the dorms, though.

how to get there:

By bus: Call hostel for transit route.
By car: Call hostel for directions.
By train: Train station in Dublin; call hostel for transit route.

litton lane hostel

2–4 Litton Lane, Dublin

Phone Number: 01–872–8389
Fax Number: 01–872–0039
Rates: €15–€25 per person (about $15–$25 US); doubles €60–€80 (about $60 to $80 US)
Credit cards: Yes
Beds: 96
Private/family rooms: Yes
Kitchen available: Yes
Office hours: Twenty-four hours
Affiliation: IHH
Extras: TV lounge, laundry, Internet access ($)

Talk about location—and history. This hostel sits right on the River Liffey, in the thick of things, a short walk from most any part of downtown Dublin you're interested in. And it used to be a recording studio where frickin' *U2* laid down tracks back before they went all techno (not that there's anything wrong with that), not to mention Vanbc—oops, Van Morrison.

Gestalt: You, too

Party index:

They've got the standard bunkrooms, of course, but also some pretty nifty apartments and private rooms. The apartments cost in the $100 range, but they're worth it; all come with access to special family-friendly amenities like a laundry and kitchen.

how to get there:

By bus: From Busarus station, walk 1/4 mile along Abbey Street or along river to O'Connell Bridge; hostel is just past bridge, on right, down Litton Lane.

By car: Contact hostel for directions.

By train: From Connelly Station, walk 300 yards to river, turn right, and continue about 1/3 mile to O'Connell Bridge. Hostel is just past bridge, on right, down Litton Lane.

marlborough hostel

81-82 Marlborough Street, Dublin 1

Phone Number: 01–874–7629
Fax: 01–874–5172
E-mail: mail@marlboroughhostel.com
Rates: €11.50–€19.00 per person (about $11.50–$19.00 US); doubles €56–€64 (about $56–$64 US)
Credit cards: Yes
Beds: 76
Private/family rooms: Yes
Kitchen available: Yes
Office hours: Twenty-four hours
Affiliation: IHH
Extras: Breakfast, laundry, grill, bike rentals, sheets ($), storage

A nicely scrubbed and painted brick facility, this hostel's a fine option when in Dublin. It's quite close to the central attractions of the city, staff and crowd are cool, and the usual ten-bed bunkrooms don't feel too bad. However, communal showers segregated by sex aren't for the shy.

Gestalt: Marlborough men

Safety:

Cleanliness:

Party index:

Three private rooms are up for grabs, and all get a small breakfast plus use of the common room and kitchen combo.

how to get there:

By bus: Bus station in Dublin; call hostel for transit route.

By car: From O'Connell Street, go north to North Earl, then turn right onto Marlborough; hostel is on left.

By train: Train station in Dublin; call hostel for transit route.

mount eccles court hostel

45 North Great Georges Street, Dublin 1, Co. Dublin

Phone Number: 01–873–0826
Fax: 01–878–3554
E-mail: meccles@iol.ie
Rates: €13–€30 (about $13–$30 US); doubles €56–€84 (about $56–$84 US)
Credit cards: Yes
Beds: 115
Private/family rooms: Yes
Season: January 3 to December 24
Office hours: Twenty-four hours
Affiliation: IHH
Extras: Breakfast, free parking

This eighteenth-century Georgian convent is semicentral, and they seem to have outfitted with the right stuff—a mixture of various sizes of dorms and private and double rooms. Reports indicate that the place is well made up, and hostellers lauded the inclusion of breakfast. (But don't they always?)

Gestalt: Nun too soon

Safety:

Cleanliness:

Party index:

The James Joyce Center is practically next door. Otherwise, you're gonna hafta hoof it a little bit to get to the other sites, pubs, and so forth in town.

how to get there:

By bus: Contact hostel for transit route.
By car: Contact hostel for directions.
By train: Contact hostel for transit route.

oliver st. john gogarty's temple bar hostel

18-21 Anglesea Street, Dublin

Phone Number: 01–671–1822
Fax: 01–671–7637
E-mail: info@olivergogartys.com
Rates: €15–€30 per person (about $15–$30 US); doubles €66–€80 (about $66–$80 US)
Kitchen available: No
Affiliation: IHH

The single reason for staying at this hostel is the super location, a double whammy of good luck: One, it's in Temple Bar. Two, it's next to a pub with the same name as the hostel. So you can drown your sorrows if you don't like the bunks.

And, frankly, you might not. They come packed six or eight or more to a room and are only so-so at best. At least dorms have their own bathrooms. The private apartments here aren't really part of the hostel and cost a lot more—upward of €100 (about $100 US) for a quad—but they do offer more amenities.

Gestalt: Beer and now
Hospitality:
Cleanliness:
Party Index:

how to get there:

By bus: Call hostel for transit route.
By car: Call hostel for directions.
By train: Call hostel for transit route.

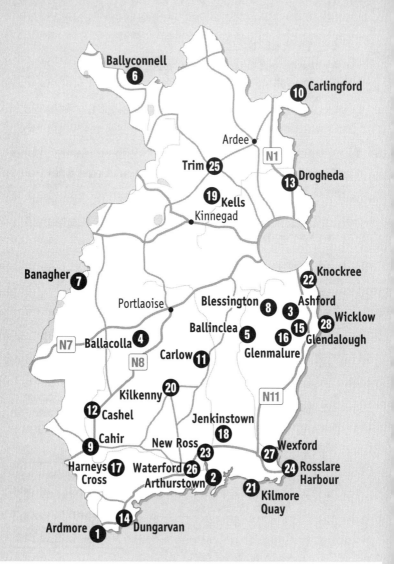

Ballyconnell 6

Carlingford 10

Ardee

N1

Trim 25

13 Drogheda

19 Kells
Kinnegad

Banagher 7

22 Knockree

Portlaoise

Blessington 8 3 Ashford
28 Wicklow
Ballinclea 5 15
N7 Ballacolla 4 16 Glendalough
N8 Carlow 11 Glenmalure

20
Kilkenny
12 Cashel
Jenkinstown
18
Cahir
9 New Ross N11
17 23 27 Wexford
Harneys Waterford 26 24 Rosslare
Cross Arthurstown 2 Harbour
21
14 Kilmore
Ardmore 1 Dungarvan Quay

eastern ireland

Eastern Ireland is often skipped over by travelers hell-bent for the west coast. But this lack of attention has actually helped to keep certain pockets of the east interesting. (Towns near Dublin, unfortunately, are succumbing to suburban sprawl.)

Many of the hostels here are small, rustic affairs, sometimes located on farms; think low party factor, but huge lungfuls of fresh air. Also, this is the sunniest part of Ireland, so take advantage of that.

Once you've landed in Dublin, it's not far to the surrounding counties—some, in fact, can even be reached with the DART bus and train system that serves the greater Dublin area. Many of these smallish villages are popular with local tourists, and with good reason: They often come with their own castles, some of which have been transformed into arts centers, recording studios, or other strange (yet strangely appropriate) uses.

To get to other destinations in the east, try taking a ferry from Wales or England; you might land in Wexford or Waterford, attractive and somewhat working-class counties with plenty of ocean frontage and old ruins.

key to icons

Attractive natural setting	Comfortable beds	Good for active travelers
Ecologically aware hostel	A particularly good value	Visual arts at hostel or nearby
Superior kitchen facilities or cafe	Wheelchair accessible	Music at hostel or nearby
Offbeat or eccentric place	Good for business travelers	Great hostel for skiers
Superior bathroom facilities	Especially well suited for families	Bar or pub at hostel or nearby
Romantic private rooms		Editors' choice: among our very favorite hostels

---

ardmore beach hostel

Main Street, Ardmore, Co. Waterford

Phone Number: 024–94166
Rates: €13–€14 (about $13–$14 US) per person; doubles €34 (about $34 US)
Private/family rooms: Yes
Affiliation: None
Extras: Laundry

This place scores big in comfort, but the architecture's blah. Luckily,

Insiders' tip: St. Declan's Monastery

Gestalt: Ard way

Party index:

the hostel maintains one superb (though quite expensive) private room. We even hesitate to call it a room, as it's more like renting your own ski lodge for the night. Well, something like that.

As is usual in this little-visited corner of the Waterford-Cork border, the sea cliffs are the prime attraction. Plenty of ruins related to old St. Declan—a legendary figure in Irish history—are here, too; check out his well, for starters.

how to get there:

By bus: Call hostel for transit route.
By car: Call hostel for directions.
By train: Call hostel for transit route.

arthurstown hostel

Coastguard Station, Arthurstown, New Ross, Co. Wexford

Phone Number: 051–389–411
Rates: €11.00–€13.50 per HI member (about $11.00–$13.50 US)
Credit cards: None
Beds: 30
Private/family rooms: Yes
Kitchen available: Yes
Office hours: 7:00 to 10:00 A.M.; 5:00 P.M. to midnight
Season: June 1 to September 30
Curfew: 10:30 P.M.
Affiliation: HI-AO
Lockout: 10:00 A.M. to 5:00 P.M.

Located in a former lifesaving station on the Hook Head Peninsula, this hostel's plain, but the views are great. Get ready for teeny dorm rooms, though; two have four beds, two have two beds, and six have three beds apiece.

There's a historical site about 10 miles away: Baginbun, the spot where the first Norman invaders made landfall in Ireland and began wreaking havoc way back in the eleventh century. Or, for a more bourgeois

Gestalt: Coaster
Cleanliness:
Party Index:

pleasure, you might take a ferry (so can your car) across the Suir River to Waterford and tour its crystal factory.

how to get there:

By bus: From Waterford, take Suirway Bus to Passage East (runs until 6:00 P.M.) and take ferry to Ballyhack; walk 1 mile to hostel.
By car/ferry: From Waterford, take Suirway Ferry from Waterford to Passage East, then drive 1 mile to hostel.
By train: Campile Station is 5 miles away.

tiglin hostel

Devil's Glen, Ashford, Co. Wicklow

Phone Number: 0404–49049
Fax: 0404–49049
E-mail: tiglinyouthhostel@go.com
Rates: €10–€13 per HI member (about $10–$13 US)
Credit cards: None
Beds: 50
Private/family rooms: Yes
Office hours: 7:00 to 10:30 A.M.; 5:00 P.M. to midnight
Affiliation: HI-AO
Extras: Store

A farmhouse built in 1870, this hostel has a quite pleasant setting in a state forest; the National Outdoor Training Centre is next door, with a walking trail in between. There's a ten-bed dorm, three eight-bed dorms, and one quad room. Deer are often seen in the woods, and an outdoor sculpture garden gives hostellers something to do during the day if you're stranded without wheels or the will to go walking in Devil's Glen State Forest.

Gestalt: Devil may care

Party index:

A small store inside the hostel dispenses simple foods, and you might need it—it's a bit of a hike, more than an hour, out to civilization. At least the adventure center gives you a chance to engage in more extreme pursuits.

how to get there:

By bus: From Dublin, take bus toward Waterford or Rosslare Harbour to Ashford; get off at Ashford and walk 3½ miles to hostel.
By car: Take N11 from Dublin to Ashford, then follow signs to hostel.
By train: Wicklow Station, 7 miles away, is closest.

traditional farm hostel

Farren House, Ballacolla, Co. Laois

Phone Number: 0502–34032
Fax: 0502–34008

Rates: €12.50 per person (about $12.50 US); doubles €25 (about $25 US)
Beds: 35
Private/family rooms: Yes
Affiliation: IHH
Extras: Meals ($), breakfast, camping, laundry, bike rentals, pickups

This place epitomizes what rustic hostelling is all about: It's located in the grain loft of an organic farm, and the focus here is on country living and the food. (How many times have we seen this in Ireland?)

> **Gestalt:** Salad days
> **Hospitality:**
> **Party index:**

Meals are available, and they're pretty darned good. Four private rooms take the edge off communal living.

how to get there:

By bus: Free pickups available; call hostel for details.
By car: From Durrow, drive 2 miles northwest on R434.
By train: Free pickups available; call hostel for details.

ballinclea hostel

Ballinclea, Donard, Co. Wicklow

Phone Number: 045–404657
Fax: 045-404657
Rates: €11–€13 per HI member (about $11–$13 US)
Credit cards: None
Beds: 34
Private/family rooms: No
Kitchen available: Yes
Season: March 1 to November 30, daily; December 1 to February 28, weekends only
Office hours: 7:00 to 10:00 A.M.; 5:00 P.M. to midnight
Affiliation: HI-AO
Extras: Fireplace
Lockout: 10:00 A.M. to 5:00 P.M.

Another simple base for exploring the Wicklow Mountains, this white-washed farmhouse is closest to Lugnaquilla, highest among the bunch.

There are just four rooms here—two ten-bed dorms, an eight-bed room, and a six-bed room. A large fireplace adds warmth and atmosphere; orienteering and horseback riding are available close by the hostel if you're into them. But most hostellers here are either coming to walk the Wicklows or else escaping from Dublin for a rustic weekend.

Cleanliness:
Party index:

how to get there:

By bus: From Dublin, take Bus Eireann toward Baltinglass to Donard or Annelecky Cross, then walk 3 miles to hostel.
By car: Call hostel for directions.
By train: Newbridge Station, 21 miles away, is closest stop.

sandville house hostel

Ballyconnell, Co. Cavan

Phone Number: 04995–26297
Rates: €12–€15 per person (about $12–$15 US)
Beds: 30
Private/family rooms: 2
Affiliation: IHO
Extras: Bike rentals, canoe rentals, fireplace, pickups, camping, laundry

Where once were pigs, now are hostellers. Or something like that. This former barn out in the sticks couldn't be any friendlier, so if you can get way out here—and they'll even pick you up from transit points—you'll probably enjoy a nice getaway. As a bonus, they keep a fire going and maintain huge gardens. And the place is very inexpensive.

Gestalt: Great lakes
Hospitality:
Party index:

There are some great waterways around here—in fact, the larger area is known as the Fermanagh Lake District—so grab a canoe at the hostel and set out for the local inlets and coves. Or grab a bike and take the overland route. (Though the place is very close to Northern Ireland, don't sweat the border stuff if you're coming from or going toward that direction.)

The hostel's actually a distance outside Ballyconnell, but take note:

From that town, you can experience one of the weirdest (or most blissful, depending on your point of view) places in Ireland: Krishna Island, owned by devotees of you-know-who. It's kinda like spending time at a monastery—or, come to think of it, a hostel. Check it out by taking a boat.

Be forewarned that groups occasionally book the whole place up. So it's best to call before trekking all the way out here.

how to get there:

By bus: Call hostel for transit route or pickup.
By car: Call hostel for directions.
By train: Call hostel for transit route.

crank house hostel

Main Street, Banagher, Co. Offaly

Phone Number: 0902–57561
E-mail: abguinan@eircom.net
Rates: €11 per person (about $11 US)
Beds: 40
Private/family rooms: Yes
Affiliation: IHH
Extras: Coffee shop ($), laundry, meals ($), free pickups

Not much to report here, but it's certainly adequate for your needs if you find yourself in the area. This smallish hostel includes a coffee shop and a gallery, which is nice, plus it's right next to the local tourist info desk. Dorms come two to four beds per room, a welcome switch from the prison-style bunks in some Dublin hostels, plus there's a single private room.

Insiders' tip:
Great cathedral
in Clonfert

Gestalt: Crank and file
Party index:

The town of Banagher, a small hamlet right on the goodly sized River Shannon, seems quaintly unremarkable. But wait! Anthony Trollope and Charlotte Brontë both passed through for a while. Anglophiles, go nuts.

how to get there:

By bus: Call hostel for directions.
By car: Call hostel for directions.
By train: Call hostel for directions.

baltyboys hostel

Baltyboys, Blessington, Co. Wicklow

Phone Number: 045–867–266
Fax: 045–867–032
Rates: €11–€13 per HI member (about $11–$13 US)
Credit cards: None
Beds: 34
Private/family rooms: None
Kitchen available: Yes
Office hours: 7:00 to 10:00 A.M.; 5:00 P.M. to midnight
Season: March 1 to November 30, daily; rest of the year, weekends only
Affiliation: HI-AO
Lockout: 10:00 A.M. to 5:00 P.M.

A converted schoolhouse in the woods reached by wooden stairs and railings made of branches, this hostel's best for those who want countryside ambience and access to some of Ireland's legendary fishing. There are just two monster dorms, with 18 beds apiece, nothing more private.

Gestalt: Cool school
Party index: 🎉

The hostel isn't really close to anything else of note, but it is darned cheap—and you can take a bus directly from Dublin.

how to get there:

By bus: From Dublin (Eden Quay), take 65 bus toward Ballyknockan (two daily)
By car: Call hostel for directions
By train: Newbridge Station is 15 miles away.

lisakyle hostel

Church Street, Cahir, Co. Tipperary

Phone Number: 052–41963
E-mail: seancondon@eircom.net
Rates: €12 per person (about $12 US)
Beds: 17
Private rooms: Yes
Season: March 1 to October 31
Affiliation: IHH
Extras: Pickups, camping, laundry

This joint, just a mile from IHH's national office in Cahir, is surprisingly plain considering that the chain runs such wonderful hostels. Not bad, not great; just a simple little place with slim mattresses that rates in the so-so category.

Scoring the lone private room might enhance your experience a little bit, though. And the views are certainly great.

Most folks use this hostel as a base to strike out for the Rock of Cashel, which is 11 miles away and reachable by buses. Yet Cahir itself provides some fine medieval sights, as well, including the still-impressive stone city walls and an appropriately medieval-looking castle that was built back in the twelfth cen-

Gestalt: Cahir package
Hospitality:
Party Index:

tury. Cahir Castle is showing its age, but the tower and keep remain intact. A bit outside town but not too far, the Swiss Cottage's thatched roofs are also interesting.

how to get there:

By bus: Bus station is 1 mile; call hostel for directions.
By car: Call hostel for directions.
By train: Cahir Station is 1 mile; call hostel for directions.

mountain lodge hostel

Burncourt, Cahir, Co. Tipperary

Phone Number: 052–67277
Rates: €10–€13 per HI member (about $10–$13 US)
Credit cards: None
Beds: 30

Private/family rooms: No
Kitchen available: Yes
Office hours: 7:00 to 10:00 A.M.; 5:00 P.M. to midnight
Season: March 28 to September 30
Affiliation: HI-AO

Yet another former hunting lodge, this one sits about 10 miles from the market town of Cahir.

This hostel, oddly shaped and plunked down in the woods, is simple but pleasantly rustic, located in a region of the forested Galtee Mountains. No electricity here: In fact, it's gas lamps all the way, plus some fires (that's why the little building has several chimneys). Bedding consists of a twelve-bed room, two eight-bed dorms, and a room with five beds in it.

Gestalt: Mountain goat
Hospitality:
Party index:

This isn't far from the Rock of Cashel (a car would help, though), and a trail leads to the also HI-affiliated Ballydavid Wood House hostel. It's 3 miles to a market, but that shouldn't faze you if you've made the effort to get here.

how to get there:

By bus: From Dublin or Cork, take Bus Eireann to hostel gate between Cahir and Mitchelstown. From gate, walk a mile to the hostel.
By car: Hotel is halfway between Cahir and Mitchelstown on the N8.
By train: Cahir Station is 10 miles away.

carlingford adventure centre hostel

Tholsel Street, Carlingford, Co. Louth

Phone Number: 042–73100
Fax: 042–937–3651
E-mail: info@carlingfordadventure.com
Rates: €15–€20 per person (about $15–$20 US)
Beds: 33
Private/family rooms: Yes
Season: January 15 to December 15

Affiliation: IHH
Extras: Meals ($), pickups, outings, tours, equipment rentals

---

These converted warehouses are affiliated with an outdoor adventure center, which means lots of opportunity to book classes or tours using feet, canoes, bikes, sailboards, and more.

Alas, along with these classes and trips come—sometimes—droves of schoolkids. Hang in there, though, because the dorms (containing two to eight beds apiece) aren't half bad. The great staff and their adventurous trips and tours partly—though not completely—offset the piles of kids and the too-functional architecture here.

Carlingford is an especially cute little medieval town, so this is still worth a stay if you're passing through the area. Try to make it to town for the fun summertime Leprechaun Hunt, too, which gets the townsfolk and interested hostellers out in the fresh air to track down pots of coins disguised as leprechauns in the hills.

Best bet for a bite:
Chervy's

Gestalt:
Excellent adventure

Hospitality:

Party index:

how to get there:

By bus: Call hostel for pickup.
By car: Call hostel for directions.
By train: Call hostel for transit route.

otterholt riverside hostel

Otterholt, Kilkenny Road, Carlow, Co. Carlow

Phone Number: 0503–30404
Fax: 0503–31170
Rates: €14–€15 per person (about $14–$15 US)
Beds: 39
Private/family rooms: Yes
Kitchen available: Yes
Affiliation: IHH
Extras: Camping, laundry, bike rentals, TV, grill, gardens

This 1810 Georgian House is well done up. Big gardens surround the building, which sits just a few minutes from central Carlow Town in a pretty riverside location.

The setup here includes a kitchen, outdoor grill, common room with fireplace, and a laundry. We'd opt for the campsite on the River Barrow, though, in good weather—or one of the four private rooms as a slight splurge.

Canoeing is the top draw, on three local rivers; you can store your canoe at the hostel, dry it out there, even launch it directly from the garden! Not the kind who enjoys getting wet? No problemo. The easy Barrow Way trail passes nearby, or hardcore hikers can try for the Blackstairs or Wicklow Mountains. Bikes can be rented close at hand, as well. You might wheel 2-plus miles over to Brownes Hill to check out one of the biggest ancient stone gravesites ("dolmens") in Europe.

Gestalt: Carlow budget

Party index:

Carlow Town itself is okay for a night's stop, too, with a number of pubs and live music spots.

how to get there:

By bus: From Dublin, take bus to Carlow and ask driver for drop-off at RTC campus; hostel is across road.

key to icons

 Attractive natural setting

 Ecologically aware hostel

 Superior kitchen facilities or cafe

 Offbeat or eccentric place

 Superior bathroom facilities

 Romantic private rooms

 Comfortable beds

 A particularly good value

 Wheelchair accessible

 Good for business travelers

 Especially well suited for families

 Good for active travelers

 Visual arts at hostel or nearby

 Music at hostel or nearby

 Great hostel for skiers

 Bar or pub at hostel or nearby

 Editors' choice: among our very favorite hostels

By car: From Carlow center, drive out Kilkenny Road; hostel is opposite Regional Technical College, on river.

By train: Call hostel for directions from train station.

cashel holiday hostel

6 John Street, Cashel, Co. Tipperary

Phone Number: 062–62330
Fax: 062–62445
E-mail: cashelho@iol.ie
Rates: €13 per person (about $13); doubles €36 (about $36 US)
Beds: 43
Private/family rooms: Yes
Kitchen available: Yes
Affiliation: IHH
Extras: Pickups, bike rental, laundry, meals ($), fireplace, Internet

This very good hostel serves as an excellent base for Rock of Cashel exploring—and for tasting Cashel's most famous export: Guinness beer was invented right here in the eighteenth century. (Well, not at the hostel.)

The place is bigger than the other option in town, and therefore less likely to fill up when the inevitable summer crush hits as tourists the world over scramble for position on the Rock. Good thing for you, because it's among the top-tier places in Ireland.

Best bet for a bite:
Centra Supermarket

Gestalt:
Dash for Cashel

Hospitality:

Party index:

What makes it so good? It's got character—a variety of rooms and beds, a layout that's eccentric rather than prison-block style, and actual beds to sleep in instead of piled-up bunk beds. Couple this unique architecture with a staff that knows all about the area's charms, and you've got a winner.

Three double rooms are available, which are good, and one of the extras touches here is the longer bunks for taller hostellers. The common room fireplace also gets a workout.

how to get there:

By bus: Call hostel for pickup.

By car: Hostel is downtown, 2 blocks from tourist information office.

By train: Call hostel for transit details.

o'brien's farm hostel

St. Patrick's Rock, Dundrum Road, Cashel, Co. Tipperary

Phone Number: 062–61003
Fax: 062–61003
Rates: €13–€15 per person (about $13–$15 US)
Beds: 23
Private/family rooms: Yes
Affiliation: IHH
Extras: Laundry, bike rental, camping, free pickups, sheets included

Just across the road from an abbey and practically underneath the famous Rock of Cashel, you couldn't get closer if you tried. This place is a stone barn with attached coach house, and though small, it does include three private rooms and stunning views. It's another winner within spitting distance of the Rock.

Best bet for a bite:
SuperValu grocery store

Gestalt: Rock of ages

Cleanliness:

Party index:

The Rock itself—an entire little village perched on a huge stone that has no business being here in the middle of green pastures—is mighty impressive. Don't even think of skipping a trip up top. On top of this impressive limestone block, you'll find a castle, a chapel, a round tower, a cathedral, and even a choral hall.

how to get there:

By bus: Bus station in town. Call hostel for pickup.

By car: In Cashel, take Main Street to bottom; turn right just after Dundrum Road.

By train: From Cahir Station, buses run to Cashel; call hostel for transit route.

harpur house tourist hostel

William Street, Drogheda, Co. Louth

Phone Number: 041–9832736
Fax: 041–9832736
Rates: €12.50–€15.00 per person (about $12.50–$15.00 US)
Beds: 16
Private/family rooms: Yes
Affiliation: IHO
Extras: Breakfast ($)

Set in a compact but nice town on the River Boyne, this central hostel offers up a mixture of private double rooms and dorms. The beds are better than usual, and the dorm rooms are adequate; not a superior-quality place, but it's okay by us. Breakfast costs extra.

Drogheda is a port city of little interest and not usually thought of as a real destination. At least the area's rich in old ruins

Party index: 🎉🎉

and historic sites commemorating those rough-and-tumble battles between Catholics and Protestants that determined the fate of Ireland as a separate entity from England.

Also make sure to come in August for an Irish folk music festival that'll clear out the cobwebs of traveling.

how to get there:

By bus: Call hostel for transit route.
By car: Call hostel for directions.
By train: Call hostel for transit route.

dungarvan holiday hostel

Youghal Road, Dungarvan, Co. Waterford

Phone Number: 058–44340
Fax: 052–36294
Rates: €14–€16 per person (about $14–$16 US); doubles €34–€38 (about $34–$38 US)
Beds: 52
Private/family rooms: Yes
Affiliation: IHH
Extras: Bike rentals, meals ($), camping

There are several good beaches near this rustic monastery-turned-hostel, which features five private rooms and such amenities as a camping area and bikes for hire.

Not super, just basically a place to hang out and enjoy the good scenery. The special-abled can stay here and sample the fresh air, too, as the hostel's outfitted for wheelchair access, but rooms are pretty smallish. Its close proximity to the police station could possibly be counted as a plus—unless you're looking to do some mischief, in which case it's the pits.

Best bet for a bite:
L&N Superstore

Insiders' tip:
Big Music Festival in May

Party index: 🎉

how to get there:

By bus: Off Emmet Street near Garda HQ (cops), direction Cork.
By car: Call hostel for directions.
By train: Call hostel for transit route.

glendalough lodge hostel

Glendalough, Co. Wicklow

Phone Number: 0404–45342
Fax: 0404–45690
E-mail: glendalough@ireland.com
Rates: €14.00–€20.50 per HI member (about $14.00–$21.00 US)
Credit cards: Yes
Beds: 120
Private/family rooms: Yes
Office hours: 7:00 to 10:30 A.M.; 5:00 P.M. to midnight
Affiliation: HI-AO
Extras: Laundry, Internet access, bike rentals, bureau de change, IBN
Curfew: 11:00 P.M.

Spruced up and reopened in July 1998, An Oige's Glendalough joint enjoys position close to some of Ireland's most revered ruins—the sixth-century monastery that's now a stunning little national park (and national treasure to the Irish). Too bad the town's gotten so touristy.

Despite the fix ups, the dorms here are still not the most thrilling in the world. All rooms now include en-suite bathrooms; you'll pay extra for the doubles and quads, of course, but it might well be worth it as the dorm bunks are pretty iffy—not so comfortable. There are two eight-bed dorms, seven six-bed rooms, fourteen quad rooms, and three double rooms.

Gestalt:
Hodgepodge lodge

Cleanliness:

Party index:

The kitchen's pretty good, too, and it's just a mile to the village of Laragh for a market where you can stock up on supplies.

Of course, don't miss the ruins. They're a simple complex of stone buildings established around A.D. 500 by a guy called St. Kevin. (More about him elsewhere in these pages.) It's an enormously popular sight for visitors. If you can find room to breathe, check out the pointy round tower and then look over the intriguing stone crosses scattered about the site.

how to get there:

By bus: From St. Stephen's Green in Dublin, take St. Kevins Coach to Glendalough Park; turn left at visitor center, walk across river and continue ¼ mile.

By car: Follow signs for Glendalough Monastic settlement. Hostel is on road to upper lake.

By train: Rathdrum Station is 8 miles away.

old presbytery hostel

The Fairgreen, Rathdrum, Glendalough, Co. Wicklow

Phone Number: 0404–46930
Fax: 0404–46604
E-mail: theoldpres@eircom.net
Rates: €13 per person (about $13 US)
Credit cards: Yes
Beds: 55
Private/family rooms: Yes
Affiliation: None
Extras: Camping, laundry, bike rentals, sheets, Internet access

A weatherbeaten farmhouse in the hills near the Glendalough ruins,

Best bet for a bite:	Woolpack Pub
Insiders' tip:	Cartoon-themed pub in town
Gestalt:	Toon town
Cleanliness:	
Party index:	

this is probably not as good an option as the HI-affiliated joint in town. However, it's only an hour's walk from the park, and the surrounding scenery is nice. Also, it's surely less hectic than the An Oige joint. Six beds fill most rooms.

The big event of the year around here is the annual cartoon festival (don't ask us why it's here; we've no idea) late each spring. You will definitely need an advance booking then, but any other time of year the place should be wide open. There's also a good park in town; it's on the river and attached to a museum of sorts, to which you must unfortunately pay admission.

how to get there:

By bus: Take St. Kevin's Coach from St. Stephen's Green in Dublin to Glendalough Park; leaving visitor center, walk right on main road and follow signs to hostel.

By car: Call hostel for directions.

By train: Rathdrum Station is closest; call hostel for directions.

glenmalure hostel

Glenmalure, Greenane, Co. Wicklow

No Phone; book through An Oige lead office (01–830–4555)
Rates: €10–€13 per HI member (about $10–$13 US)
Credit cards: None
Beds: 16
Private/family rooms: None
Kitchen available: Yes
Office hours: 7:00 to 10:30 A.M. 5:00 to 11:00 P.M.
Season: June 24 to August 31; Saturday nights only, rest of year
Affiliation: HI-AO

No phone, no electricity, no problem. That's what we say about this rusticating joint, a handsome if simple two-story house nestled at the head of a beautiful valley. You'll get to know that valley well: To get here, you must walk 4 miles up a trail beside the river, which flows over rocks right through the front yard of the hostel. Cool.

Once here, the gaslit cottage provides an intimate and pleasant enough experience. Catch trout in the brook, or pack something else in, because there's no food for acres. What there is, is a whole lot of time to think about things—and to walk around on any of a number of trails thinking about them some more. Afterward, bed down in one of two snug rooms: one has ten beds, the other six.

Gestalt: Simply the best

Party index: 🎉

Remember that the hostel's only open full-time in summer—and that you don't want to go poking around in the war games practice range nearby.

how to get there:

By bus: Take St. Kevins Coach from Stephens Green in Dublin (two daily) to Laragh, 9 miles away. Follow Wicklow Way to Drumgoff Bridge, turn up Glenmalure Valley and continue to hostel.

By car: Write hostel for directions.

By foot: Hostel is 4 miles up valley from trail at Drumgoff Bridge. Write hostel for directions.

By train: Take train to Rathdrum Station, 10 miles away; contact An Oige for transit route.

powers the pot hostel caravan park

Harneys Cross, Clonmel, Co. Waterford

Phone Number: 052–23085
Rates: Contact hostel for rates
Private/family rooms: Yes
Season: Contact hostel for season
Affiliation: None
Extras: Pickups, restaurant ($), bar, laundry, camping

A big house with an actual thatched roof, this is one of Ireland's best small home hostels. At press time, repairs were ongoing, but you could still camp here; call for an update if you're planning to bunk down here.

Best bet for a bite:
The Honey Pot

Gestalt: Pot luck

Hospitality:

Cleanliness:

Party index:

Your impression starts with incredible views of the hills and lowlands from the yard, and it just gets better: The owners are friendly; they serve meals and pour drinks at the bar and restaurant, and maintain super beds (as opposed to uncomfy bunks). The attached campground adds to the fun. And, yeah, they'll pick you up.

how to get there:

By bus: Call hostel for transit route.
By car: Call hostel for directions.
By train: Call hostel for transit route.

foulksrath castle hostel

Jenkinstown, Co. Kilkenny

Phone Number: 056–67674
Fax: 056–67144
Rates: €11–€13 per HI member (about $11–$13 US)
Credit cards: None
Beds: 52
Private/family rooms: None
Kitchen available: Yes
Office hours: 7:00 to 10:00 A.M.; 5:00 P.M. to midnight
Lockout: 10:00 A.M. to 5 P.M.
Affiliation: HI-AO
Extras: TV, laundry
Curfew: 10:30 P.M.

You see this old castle with greenery hanging all over it in a tiny Irish village, and you get excited. Wow! I'm in Europe! you think. Pinch me!

It's a fifteenth-century castle, that's for sure, with authentic touches Disney could never fake, like a tower, feasting hall, huge fireplaces, and a spiral staircase leading to the upper floors. It's a downright impressive sight that became a hostel way back in 1938, Ireland's very first, when the bloom on world hostelling was still fresh and new.

To be honest, though, this place isn't as great on the inside as it is on the outside. In fact, dorm rooms—containing twelve, eighteen, and twenty-two beds, respectively—can be cold, echoey, and not so comfortable. On the other hand, come to think of it, that's the way real castles were. And recent improvements like a TV lounge have made it homier than ever. So think of it as an experiment in medieval living, and you'll be okay.

Though a bit remote from town, you can take a local bus service from Kilkenny to or from the hostel twice a day. Most folks here don't hang around

Gestalt: King sized
Party Index:

little Jenkinstown. Instead, they make for the local Dunmore Caves or negotiate the 8-mile trip into Kilkenny Town for music and other cultural stuff.

how to get there:

By bus: From Kilkenny Castle, bus stops at Conahy Cross, 1 mile away; call 056–41264 for transit details.
By car: Call hostel for directions.
By train: Kilkenny Station is 8 miles away.

key to icons

 Attractive natural setting

 Ecologically aware hostel

 Superior kitchen facilities or cafe

 Offbeat or eccentric place

 Superior bathroom facilities

 Romantic private rooms

 Comfortable beds

 A particularly good value

 Wheelchair accessible

Good for business travelers

 Especially well suited for families

 Good for active travelers

Visual arts at hostel or nearby

Music at hostel or nearby

Great hostel for skiers

 Bar or pub at hostel or nearby

Editors' choice: among our very favorite hostels

kells hostel

Carrick Street, Kells, Co. Meath

Phone Number: 046–49995
Fax: 046–40683
E-mail: hostels@iol.ie
Rates: €13 per person (about $13 US); doubles €32 (about $32 US)
Credit cards: V, MC
Beds: 30
Private/family rooms: Yes
Kitchen available: Yes
Office hours: 9:00 A.M. to noon; 5:00 to 10:00 P.M.
Affiliation: IHH
Extras: Laundry, meals ($), pool table, tours, gym, squash courts, bike rentals, Internet, TV, sheets, camping

The main amenity here is the proximity to beer, company, and the steep, interesting street on which the hostel lies. You check in at the pub, in fact, and will probably hang out there awhile quaffing stout or ogling a replica of the ultrafamous Book of Kells.

Yeah, that's right—this village is the place where monks worked

Gestalt: Kell's Bells
Hospitality:
Party index:

over the illuminated manuscript of the Book (though it originated in the islands to the west and now resides in Dublin). Therefore, St. Columba's Church—where they did the deed, and where a copy still remains—is obviously the first place you're going to visit after the pub.

But that's not all you can see here. Also take one of the good tours offered by the hostel and/or scale the impressive tower that gives tremendous views of the surrounding countryside. During the right time in summer, you could even check out an annual festival that gets Kells jumping at last.

All in all, this hostel is not too bad if you don't mind the noise, smoke, and other tangential hazards of trying to sleep above a bar. There are nine private rooms, too. Kells itself isn't nearly as inspiring as the Book, of course, but how could it be?

how to get there:

By bus: Call hostel for transit route.

By car: Call hostel for directions.
By train: Call hostel for transit route.

kilkenny tourist hostel

35 Parliament Street, Kilkenny, Co. Kilkenny

Phone Number: 056–63541
Fax: 056–23397
E-mail: kilkennyhostel@eircom.net
Rates: €13–€14 per person (about $13–$14 US); doubles €34–€36 (about $34–$36 US)
Beds: 60
Kitchen available: Yes
Affiliation: IHH
Extras: Laundry

Right in downtown Kilkenny, this unpretentious and incredibly sociable place supplies two of our basic daily requirements of good hostelling: Staff is friendly, and it's kept clean. It's an attractive building, too, handsome and well maintained. You'll especially enjoy eating in the dining room—and saving oodles over the B&Bs in town.

The town itself—stuffed with old churches, a castle, and pubs galore—makes a perfect intro course to Olde Eire. The central attraction here is probably Kilkenny Castle. Surrounded by parks, the castle was built way back in the roaring 1100s; today, it's still impressive although a bit squat.

Best bet for a bite: Superquinn
Gestalt: Kilkenny G
Cleanliness:
Hospitality:
Party index:

Some of the best drinking houses in town are just steps away on Parliament Street, or just around some other fetching corner. Try pub crawling from Parliament over to nearby Langton's, the Marble Bar, and Kyteler's, and you'll never want to leave.

If you can still stand.

how to get there:

By bus: From bus station, turn left on John Street, cross river, then turn right on Kieran or High to Parliament.

By car: Call hostel for directions.
By train: From Kilkenny Station, turn left on John Street, cross river, then turn right on Kieran or High to Parliament.

kilturk hostel

Kilmore Quay, Co. Wexford

Phone Number: 053–29883
Fax: 053–29522
Rates: €15 per person (about $15 US)
Beds: 25
Private/family rooms: Yes
Season: May 1 to October 1
Affiliation: None
Extras: Meals ($), camping, laundry, pickups, bike rentals, boat tours

This place is mellow and fairly well equipped, with its own cafe for hanging out and five private rooms for families. Not on the beaten track, not at all, but sometimes that's what you want—access to tiny fishing villages and beaches.

Gestalt: Kilturkey
Hospitality:
Party Index:

Unfortunately, the hostel could still be a lot better. Comfort isn't really a priority here, so you might spend more time than planned out and about. Good thing the management offers boat tours of the nearby Saltee Islands.

how to get there:

By car: Call hostel for directions.
By train: Call hostel for transit route.

lacken house hostel

Knockree, Enniskerry, Co. Wicklow

Phone Number: 01–286–4036
Rates: €9.00–€12.00 per HI member (about $9.00–$12.00 US)
Credit cards: None

Beds: 58
Private/family rooms: None
Kitchen available: Yes
Office hours: 7:00 to 10:00 A.M.; 5:00 P.M. to midnight
Affiliation: HI-AO
Extras: Fireplace
Lockout: 10:00 A.M. to 5:00 P.M.

An eighteenth-century stone farmhouse in the village of Knockree, this hostel is simple as pie but certainly will do: The brook running alongside tells you that you're out in the sticks to relax, as do the lawns and a few shade trees. A fireplace and kitchen within are about the only creature comforts; dorms contain six, eight, and (in two cases) sixteen beds each.

Gestalt: Slacken House
Party index:

key to icons

 Attractive natural setting

 Ecologically aware hostel

 Superior kitchen facilities or cafe

 Offbeat or eccentric place

 Superior bathroom facilities

 Romantic private rooms

 Comfortable beds

 A particularly good value

 Wheelchair accessible

Good for business travelers

Especially well suited for families

 Good for active travelers

 Visual arts at hostel or nearby

 Music at hostel or nearby

Great hostel for skiers

 Bar or pub at hostel or nearby

 Editors' choice: among our very favorite hostels

Walking is the main thing here, with hills all around. You're near the Wicklow Way, so make a point of checking out the cool Powerscourt waterfall not far away.

how to get there:

By bus: From Dublin, take 44 bus to Enniskerry and walk 4½ miles to hostel. From Bray, take 185 bus to Shop River, 2 miles away.

By car: Call hostel for directions.

By train: From Bray DART Station, walk 6 miles to hostel or take Alpine Coach to Barnmire (summer only) and walk the ¼ mile from bus stop.

macmurrough farm hostel

MacMurrough, New Ross, Co. Wexford

Phone Number: 051–421–383
E-mail: hostel@macmurrough.com
Rates: €11–€14 per person (about $11–$14 US); doubles €28–€32 (about $28–$32 US)
Credit cards: Yes
Beds: 18
Private/family rooms: Yes
Season: March 1 to November 30
Affiliation: IHH
Extras: Laundry, sheets included

A small cottage outside the small but touristed town of New Ross, this hostel comes highly recommended by our snoops.

Gestalt: JFKozy
Hospitality:
Party index:

They liked the staff and the availability of a laundry, as well as the opportunity to crash in such rustic surroundings. They don't rent bicycles here, but you still ought to try cruising the local hills and valleys if you can find one in New Ross.

The main thing (maybe the only thing) here in New Ross is JFK. Yeah, that JFK. Some of President Kennedy's forebears came from this town—and you won't be able to get away from that famous visage while here. It's a virtual industry in itself.

South of the town, on the R733 road, the John F. Kennedy Arboretum gathers exotic plants and trees beside a lake—then adds a tearoom for warming up. So that's a more interesting day trip than the tourist tack, if you can find a lift.

how to get there:

By bus: Call hostel for transit route.
By car: Call hostel for directions.
By train: Call hostel for transit route.

rosslare harbour hostel

Goulding Street, Rosslare Harbour, Co. Wexford

Phone Number: 053–33399
Fax: 053–33624
E-mail: rosslareyh@oceanfree.net
Rates: €12.00–€15.50 per HI member (about $12.00–$15.50 US)
Credit cards: Yes
Beds: 68
Private/family rooms: Yes
Kitchen available: Yes
Office hours: 7:00 A.M. to midnight
Affiliation: HI-AO
Lockout: 10:00 A.M. to 5:00 P.M.
Curfew: Midnight

Convenience is everything with this whitewashed hostel: It's set on a hill overlooking Rosslare's ferry port, which is the only thing in Rosslare you could ever want or need to see. Sure, there are miles of sandy beaches and amusements around town, but there's no reason to linger with the rest of glorious Ireland awaiting. Use this hostel simply as a crash pad on your way in or out of the ferry.

It's not even that great a crash pad, really—tight quarters, purely functional architecture, and they charge for sheets. That said, the staff does try to help you out, keeping special middle-of-the-night desk hours to accommodate

Gestalt: Ross lair
Party index: 🎉🎉

bleary (and possibly seasick) ferry-goers heading to or coming from France or Wales. Dorms contain two, four, or six beds each. Big windows let in sunlight and the expansive views, and you just might get lost awhile in this rambling house—if you can get beyond the other problems.

Just don't miss your ferry, okay?

how to get there:

By bus: From harbor, walk ½ mile uphill to hostel via steps.

By ferry: From Le Havre or Cherbourg, France (twenty-four hours), or Pembroke, Wales (4½ hours), take Irish Ferries; from Fishguard, Wales, take Stena Line ferry (three hours).

By train: Rosslare Harbour Station is ½ mile; climb hill via steps to Hotel Rosslare and cross road.

bridge street tourist hostel

Bridge Street, Trim, Co. Meath

Phone Number: 046–31848
Fax: 04605–67864
E-mail: silvertrans@eircom.net
Rates: €15–€20 per person (about $15–$20 US)
Beds: 20
Private/family rooms: Yes
Affiliation: IHH
Curfew: 1:00 A.M.

This hostel's good, if simple—a combination that works over and over in Ireland. There is a curfew, but you can at least look forward to breakfast and the possibility of renting a bicycle at the front desk.

Trim Castle has always been a pretty popular stop, but after Mel Gibson shot Braveheart here, its popularity skyrocketed. (Never mind that the movie was about Scotland.) It's one of the biggest castles in a country that's chock-full of 'em, so get up there and check it out. You won't need any directions—just head for that big stone thing.

Gestalt: Fit and Trim
Party Index: 🎉🎉

how to get there:

By bus: From Dublin, take Bus Eireann to Trim and walk to river.
By car: Call hostel for directions.
By train: Call hostel for transit route.

waterford hostel

70 Manor Street, Waterford, Co. Waterford

Phone Number: 051–850–163
Fax: 051–872–064
Rates: €9.00–€13.00 per person (about $9.00–$13.00 US)
Beds: 20
Private/family rooms: Yes
Affiliation: IHH

This one's a middle-of-the-road pick in Waterford. Definitely call these guys before you ring up any of the skanky joints in town (you'll know 'em when you see 'em).

It's not huge, but the staff does a good job keeping it in shape. And you won't feel lost in the shuffle.

Hospitality:
Cleanliness:
Party index:

how to get there:

By bus: Call hostel for transit route.
By car: Call hostel for directions.
By train: Call hostel for transit route.

kirwan house

3 Mary Street, Wexford Town, Co. Wexford

Phone Number: 053–21208
E-mail: Kirwanhostel@eircom.net
Rates: €13.00–€14.50 per person (about $13.00–$14.50 US); doubles €32–€40 (about $32–$40 US)
Beds: 35
Private/family rooms: Yes
Season: February 1 to December 8
Affiliation: IHH
Extras: Laundry, bike rentals

Surprisingly, this is the lone hostel entry in Wexford—and it's certainly

Hospitality:
Party index:

adequate, with enough beds to handle families, small groups, and solitary hostellers with ease. They rent bikes and maintain a next-door laundry.

Wexford itself is a cooler little city than you'd think, with pubs, surprisingly good restaurants, ancient ruins, narrow streets, and plenty of arts. Naturalist hostellers will want to scoot over to the nearby Wexford Wildfowl Reserve, a haven for geese, swans, and like-winged creatures.

how to get there:

By bus: Call hostel for transit route.
By car: Call hostel for directions.
By train: Call hostel for transit route.

wicklow bay hostel

Marine House, The Murrough, Wicklow, Co. Wicklow

Phone Number: 0404–69213 or 0404–61174
Fax: 0404–66456
E-mail: info@wicklowbayhostel.com
Rates: €13–€14 per person (about $13–$14 US); doubles €32–€34 (about $32–$34 US)
Credit cards: Yes
Beds: 66
Private/family rooms: Yes
Season: February 1 to November 30
Affiliation: IHH
Extras: Bike rentals, laundry, pickups

Well placed near the Wicklows and other east Ireland destinations, this

Party index:

place seems to be getting better with time. You can rent a bike, and, yeah, they've got private rooms. It's happy

and well-kept and possesses terrific vistas of the surrounding area.

how to get there:

By bus: Call hostel for pickup.
By car: Call hostel for directions.
By train: Call hostel for pickup.

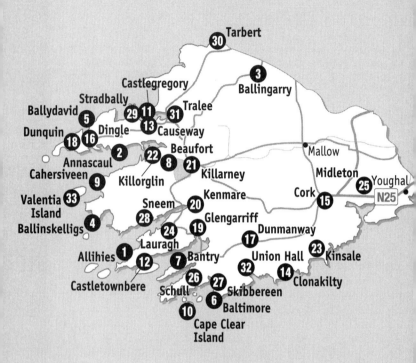

southwestern ireland

It's hard to use too many superlatives when you're here in south-western Ireland: The greenery, the hills, the rocky bays are simply jaw-dropping if you've never experienced them before.

And the hostels, well, they're just downright superb. Half of Ireland's best hostels are located in this beautiful corner of the country—places with organic farms attached, stellar restaurants, stone cottages . . . you name it. A serious back-to-the-land ethic has taken root in County Cork and thereabouts, and many of the hostels in these parts are run by non-Irish, you'll notice. The hospitality, food, and accommodations are possibly better here than anywhere else on the Emerald Isle.

Over in County Kerry, the hostels are also pretty good—if more discovered. This county's on the usual tourist itinerary, but for a reason: It's probably the best scenery in Ireland, and that's saying a lot.

Despite all these charms in the southwest, public transit can sometimes be sketchy. Trains run to Cork City—a really interesting and often-overlooked place—and supertouristed Killarney, but after that you'll need to use buses. Even those don't go everywhere all the time; you might need to rent a car or bike to see the best of the area.

Make a point of hitting one or more of the Beara, Mizen Head, Sheep's Head, Iveragh, and Dingle Peninsulas, each of which showcases not only some of Ireland's best countryside but also some of Europe's better hostelling.

allihies hostel

Cahermeelabo, Allihies, Beara Peninsula, Co. Cork

Phone Number: 027–73014
Rates: €10.00–€13.50 per HI member (about $10.00–$14.00 US)
Credit cards: None
Beds: 34
Private/family rooms: No
Kitchen available: Yes
Office hours: 7:00 to 10:00 A.M.; 5:00 P.M. to midnight
Season: June 1 to September 30
Affiliation: HI-AO
Extras: Laundry

Located among the Beara Peninsula's rugged cliffs and empty sand beaches, this place is basic and uninspiring—especially when compared with the stupendous scenery around you. It's a mile outside

Cleanliness:
Party Index:

already-tiny Allihies, if that gives you some idea about its remoteness, and, no, there's no bus or train service to get you here. If you can stand the ultrahygienic boredom of the joint, at least it's a very cheap bed. There are two ten-bed dorms, one eight-bed room, and a six-bed dorm.

Interesting stuff in the area includes a tour of the local copper mines, a cable car (hold on tight) out to Dursey Island, or a walk along the beaches of Ballydonegan.

how to get there:

By bus: From Bantry, Cork, or Killarney, summer buses run to Castletownbere, 11 miles away; call hostel for transit details.

By car: Call hostel for directions.

allihies village hostel

Main Street, Allihies, Beara Peninsula, Co. Cork

Phone Number: 027–73107
Rates: €13 per person (about $13 US)

Beds: 50
Private/family rooms: Yes
Affiliation: IHH
Extras: Bike rentals, camping, laundry, woodstove, library

Now this is more like it. Better and more homey than its companion
Allihies hostel, and also more centrally located, this recently expanded

hostel tripled its bed count and added
private rooms for good measure.
Camping is also available at an adjacent
campground.

Hospitality:
Party index:

   Management has also equipped the hostel with simple but
thoughtful touches, like frozen dinners for sale, a woodstove to keep
you warm, fresh bright paint, and a small library. Cheers for that.
   The village itself is so small and insignificant as to barely warrant a
visit; it's just a place to fuel up for "peninsulating."

how to get there:

By bus: Call hostel for transit route.
By car: Call hostel for directions.
By train: Call hostel for transit route.

fuchsia lodge hostel

Annascaul, Dingle Peninsula, Co. Kerry

Phone Number: 066–915–7150
Fax: 066–915–7402
E-mail: fuchsia@eircom.net
Rates: €12–€14 per person (about $12–$14 US); doubles €30–€36 (about
$30–$36 US)
Beds: 48
Private/family rooms: Yes
Affiliation: IHH
Extras: Meals ($), camping, laundry, bike rental, pickups, game room, shuttle,
outings, tours

Right on the Dingle Peninsula, on the way to the good stuff, this squat yellow building hides a fine, quiet hostel with an emphasis on customer service.

Dorm rooms are normal and clean. Eight private rooms, some with their own bathrooms, offer even better digs. The kitchen is nice and big; multiple cooks will have no trouble shuffling around one another fixing dinners.

Gestalt: Dingle bells
Cleanliness:
Hospitality:
Party index:

The staff here is awfully helpful, we noticed. The hostel runs a shuttle bus to the local pubs, for instance; Dingle's scene is just 10 miles away, after all. They also organize bike tours of the region or combination outings that combine walking, cycling, and shopping. They'll even help you book ahead to your next night on the road—you just pay the price of the call. All in all, a great base for Dingle explorations.

how to get there:

By bus: From Tralee or Dingle, take bus to Annascaul; walk 1 mile east to hostel or call hostel for pickup.

By car: From Tralee, take main road 17 miles toward Dingle; hostel is 1 mile east of Annascaul village.

trainor's hostel

Knight Street, Ballingarry, Co. Limerick

Phone Number: 069–68164
Fax: 069–68164
E-mail: trainorhostel@eircom.net
Rates: €14–€16 per person (about $14–$16 US); doubles €32–€36 (about $32–$36 US)
Beds: 30
Private/family rooms: Yes
Season: March 15 to September 28
Affiliation: IHH
Extras: Laundry, bike rentals

This typical IHH joint has the usual bike rental and laundry, welcome amenities both, plus two private rooms in addition to its dorms. We don't know

Party index:

much else about it, but it's probably worth a shot if you're passing through Ballingarry.

how to get there:

By bus: Call hostel for transit route.
By car: Call hostel for directions.
By train: Call hostel for transit route.

prior house

Ballinskelligs, Co. Kerry

Phone Number: 066–9479229
Rates: €11–€13 per HI member (about $11–$13 US)
Credit cards: None
Beds: 22
Private/family rooms: Yes
Kitchen available: Yes
Office hours: 7:00 to 10:00 A.M.; 5:00 P.M. to midnight
Season: March 28 to May 31, weekends only; June 1 to September 30, daily
Affiliation: HI-AO
Extras: Store

Right on the Ring of Kerry, this simple hostel is ideal for a base to hit Skellig Michael, the largest of the Skellig Rocks, with its lighthouse and monastery ruins. (You've gotta take a ferry, but it's worth it if you love rocks and ruins.)

Best bet for a bite:
on-site store

Cleanliness:

Party index:

Or check out the Skellig Heritage Museum. Nice beaches in the area, too. For chow, a tiny hostel shop does supply some dry goods.

how to get there:

By bus: From Killarney, take bus to Waterville, get off at Inny Bridge Cross, and walk 5 miles.

By car: From Ring of Kerry, turn off main road just after Sigerson Arms between Valentia Island and Waterville.

By train: Killarney Station, 50 miles away, is the closest stop.

tigh an phoist hostel

Bothar Bui, Ballydavid, Dingle, Co. Kerry

Phone Number: 066–915–5109
Fax: 066–915-5109
E-mail: s.nichon@inidgo.ie
Rates: €11–€13 per person (about $11–$13 US); doubles €32–€40 (about $32–$40 US)
Beds: 27
Private/family rooms: Yes
Season: April 1 to October 31
Affiliation: IHH
Extras: Laundry, bike rentals, hostel shop, bureau de change

On the way to Ballydavid, near the good Murreagh beach, this little hostel overlooks a harbor seemingly in the middle of nowhere. The real reason many come here is the closeness to Gallarus Observatory, one of the best old ones in the land; a little stone building, it was built in the seventh or eighth century by monks who wanted some space for private thought. Back when people did that sort of thing, ya know?

Party index:

Oh, the hostel; sorry. It's standard is as standard does, renting bikes for those Dingle rides people love to do and offering a laundry service that can be most welcome. Four private rooms are also available here.

how to get there:

By bus: Call hostel for transit route.
By car/bike: Hostel is 2 miles from Ballydavid.From Dingle Town, go along waterfront until roundabout. After bridge, make left and turn right after 250 meters. Follow signs to Muiríoch.
By train: Call hostel for transit route.

rolf's holiday hostel

Baltimore Hill, Baltimore, Co. Cork

Phone Number: 028–20289
Fax: 028–20930
Rates: €13–€15 per person (about $13–$15 US); doubles €40 (about $40 US)
Credit cards: Yes
Beds: 56
Private/family rooms: Yes
Affiliation: IHH
Extras: Meals ($), laundry, bike rentals, camping

This little hostel is one of our very favorites in Ireland, simply because it appreciates the land upon which it's built—and seeks to share that experience with others.

Best bet for a bite:
Right here

Insiders' tip:
Bike round the lake

Gestalt: German delight

Cleanliness:

Hospitality:

Party index:

Bunkrooms are a series of cottages lovingly crafted in stone and wood, each with its own austere charm. This place might get a little crowded in summer but is great otherwise. (Get one of the four private rooms, and you're all set on that count, too; everything, including the beds, is just that much nicer.)

People here are accommodating as can be, anyway, and the great common room, kitchen, and scenic dining area smooth the process of meeting and greeting fellow travelers. The staff also rents bikes and generally directs you to the spare landscape's ample charms.

And the dinners? You've got to be kidding us! Salmon? Pasta? Scones? Organic produce? Wow. We're moving here. See ya.

how to get there:

By bus: Call hostel for transit route.
By car: Call hostel for directions.

bantry independent hostel

Bishop Lucey Place, Bantry, Co. Cork

Phone Number: 027–51050
Fax: 027–151050
E-mail: bantryhostel@eircom.net
Rates: €11 per person (about $11 US); doubles €24 (about $24 US)
Beds: 30
Private/family rooms: Yes
Season: March 1 to October 30
Affiliation: IHH
Extras: Laundry, bike rental

Near (although not right in) the very prettily located town of Bantry,

Hospitality:
Party index:

this hostel has the basic requirements of hosteldom: laundry, bikes for rent, good bathrooms, and so on. Dorms have six beds each, and there are two private rooms. You'll love the sylvan location.

Bantry itself is well known for its beautiful view of Bantry Bay and the internationally famous Bantry House, expensive digs that nevertheless make nice interior sightseeing. If you're saving pennies and want more of an Irish experience, hit one of the good music pubs in town—or hike and bike your way out to the forlorn Sheep's Head Peninsula, where there won't be much more than you, rocks, grass, water, and (yeah) sheep.

how to get there:

By bus: Call hostel for transit route.
By car: Call hostel for directions.

black valley hostel

Beaufort, Killarney, Co. Kerry

Phone Number: 064–34712
Rates: €10.50–€14.00 per HI member (about $11.00–$14.00 US)
Credit cards: None

Beds: 46
Private/family rooms: Sometimes
Kitchen available: Yes
Office hours: 7:00 to 10:00 A.M.; 5:00 P.M. to midnight
Season: March 1 to November 30
Affiliation: HI-AO
Extras: Meals ($), store
Curfew: Midnight

Just a mile from the incredibly scenic Gap of Dunloe, this Hostelling International joint has good positioning. (It's also a shade more than 10 miles from Killarney, which is great if you've got a car, not so great otherwise.) They serve meals here, run a small store, and maintain family rooms.

Cleanliness:
Party index:

But things are pretty simple, so don't come expecting luxury, okay?

Serious hikers will want to hit Macgillycuddy's Reeks, or—with a car—go for the Beara Peninsula and the Ring of Kerry. An equestrian center in the area offers pony riding for a fee.

how to get there:

By bus: From Killarney or Kenmare, take Bus Éirean to Derrycunnihy and walk 4 miles through park to hostel.
By car: Take Ring of Kerry, following signs for Black Valley.
By train: Killarney Station, 13 miles away, is the closest stop.

sive hostel
15 East End, Cahersiveen, Co. Kerry

Phone Number: 066–947–2717
E-mail: sivehostel@oceanfree.net
Rates: €12–€15 per person (about $12–$15 US); doubles €30–€40 (about $30–$40 US)
Beds: 28
Private/family rooms: Yes
Affiliation: IHH
Extras: Meals ($), camping, laundry, tours

Near the village square in Cahersiveen, this place is fine as a breather on the Ring of Kerry: It's blessed with a pleasant vibe and decent

Gestalt: Sive alive

Hospitality:

Party index:

views. Dorms are normal but homey, and camping's also an option. The two private rooms are an added bonus. People like to hang out here and get to know the hostel, adding to the character of the place.

Best bet for scenery around here would be rocky, wind-torn Skellig Islands, reachable by ferry—but only in good weather.

If it's pouring cats and dogs, stick around and try to learn more about Irish hero Daniel O'Connell (known in Ireland as "the liberator"), who was born here in 1775 and helped win religious rights for Ireland's Catholics as well as other concessions from Great Britain.

Another interesting place to see would be the Barracks Heritage Centre, not only a historical exhibit but also a central fount of information about traveling around the rest of the Iveragh Peninsula area.

how to get there:

By bus: Call hostel for transit route.
By car: Call hostel for directions.
By train: Call hostel for transit route.

cape clear island hostel and adventure center

South Harbour, Cape Clear Island, Skibbereen, Co. Cork

Phone Number: 028–39198
Fax: 028–39144
E-mail: lasmuigh@eircom.net
Rates: €11.50–€14 per HI member (about $12–$14 US)
Credit cards: None
Beds: 32
Private/family rooms: Sometimes
Kitchen available: Yes
Office hours: Twenty-four hours
Season: June 1 to September 30
Affiliation: HI-AO
Extras: Outings, meeting room, laundry

Located on a small, wild island, this place gives you a taste of the real Ireland. This is a Gaeltacht—a district where Gaelic is still the primary language, and children are taught it in school as their first language. So you'll hear plenty of that tongue in the island's pub.

Best bet for a bite:
Local ice cream

Hospitality:

Cleanliness:

Pary index:

The hostel itself overlooks a fishing harbor a mile from the island's ferry dock. Although extremely plain, it now includes a wonderful new adventure center; excursions of all sorts—boat, bike, and so forth—begin here. Kudos for that, and for building this place in one of the last true bastions of Irish culture. Too bad the staff occasionally acts as though they've been sucking on sour grapes all day. Dorms contain six to ten beds each, and there are also two coveted quad rooms.

For still more fun, check out the 1,600-year-old ruins of St. Chiaran's Church near the ferry landing, home to Ireland's very first saint.

how to get there:

By car/ferry: Take ferry from Baltimore to Cape Clear Island; walk or drive 1 mile to hostel.

---

fitzgerald's eurohostel

Castlegregory, Co. Kerry

Phone Number: 06671–39133
Rates: €12 per person (about $12 US); doubles €24 (about $24 US)
Private/family rooms: Yes
Affiliation: None

When you sleep over a pub, you've got to expect the following: noise, smoke, hostellers stumbling in late at night looking for a bed (and a bedpan). And this place doesn't disappoint: It's got all that and more.

Gestalt: Beer barrel

Hospitality:

Cleanliness:

Party index:

At least the staff is friendly in a laid-back, beer-drinking way. And they've got a double room for couples. But we wouldn't bring grandma here.

how to get there:

By bus: Call hostel for transit route.
By car: Call hostel for directions.
By train: Call hostel for transit route.

garranes farmhouse hostel

Cahermore, Castletownbere, Co. Cork

Phone Number: 027–73147
Rates: €10–€20 per person (about $10–$20 US); doubles €25–€28 (about $25–$28 US)
Beds: 20
Private/family rooms: Yes
Affiliation: None
Extras: Proximity to meditation classes, laundry

Normally, a farmhouse perched on a remote seaside cliff would be a shoo-in for us when deciding where to stay the night. This place is no exception. However, there is something a little different afoot: Buddhism.

Insiders' tip:
Post office sells supplies

What hostellers say:
"Ommmmmmmm."

Gestalt: Buddha's jewel

Hospitality:

Cleanliness:

Party index:

That's right, Grasshopper. There's a Tibetan Buddhist retreat right next door, and it sometimes books the place solid. Ouch! (Camping might be allowed if you're desperate; talk to the management.) Not surprisingly, you can also often obtain free access to the meditation classes. You are, after all, in West Cork . . . simply the grooviest, greenest part of Ireland.

As for the hostel, it's a jewel worthy of the Perfected One—small, cozy, and friendly.

how to get there:

By bus: From Killarney, take Bus Éireann to Castletownbere; walk 5 miles to hostel.

By car: Hostel is 5 miles west of Castletownbere; take R572 toward Allihies, then follow sign to hostel and Buddhist Retreat Centre, ½ mile to end of road.

By train: Call hostel for transit route.

baron's bunker bar and hostel

Coast Road, Causeway, Co. Kerry

Phone Number: 066–713–1303
Fax: 066–713–1303
E-mail: baronsbunker@eircom.net
Rates: €12.50 per person (about $12.50 US); doubles €30 (about $30 US)
Credit cards: None
Beds: 21
Private/family rooms: Yes
Affiliation: IHH
Extras: Meals, laundry

We'll be darned if we know anything about this joint, in lovely County Kerry. The presence of a laundry and some meals is reason to check it out, though the tongue-twisting name (a few too many B's, guys) tripped us up a bit.

Gestalt: Red Baron
Party index: 🎉🎉

how to get there:

By bus: Call hostel for transit route.
By car: Call hostel for directions.
By train: Call hostel for transit route.

clonakilty old brewery hostel

Emmet Square, Clonakilty, Co. Cork

Phone Number: 023–33525
Fax: 023–35673
E-mail: wytchost@iol.ie
Rates: €11–€15 per person (about $11–$15 US)
Credit cards: Yes

Beds: 26
Private/family rooms: Yes
Office hours: Twenty-four hours
Affiliation: IHO
Extras: Bike rentals, laundry

This newish hostel fits the bill so far, with good bunkrooms that include sheets with the rate and a kitchen that's better than it needs to be. They rent bikes, as well, for exploring the town.

Best bet for a bite:
Brave the Black Pudding

Gestalt: Hopped up

Hospitality:

Cleanliness:

Party index:

And you'll want to explore it. You've heard this before, and now you'll hear it again: Clonakilty's the real deal, a hot spot to hear real Celtic music in real Irish pubs. A late June festival showcases some of it, but even if you can't come (or find a bed) then, the pubs keep it rolling all year long.

The beaches round here are especially nice, some of the best in Ireland.

how to get there:

By bus: Call hostel for transit route.
By car: Call hostel for directions.
By train: Call hostel for transit route.

cork

Cork is the best city in Ireland you never heard of: a place where working-class locals, brainy students, and laid-back tourists mix to the aroma of sweet stout. This downtown's got character, and you can sample it by browsing through one of the public markets or drinking at a pub.

As befits a cool town like this one, hostels here are very good. There's something for everyone—from hippie joints to parties to family-oriented places. Don't miss the local Murphy's stout, which is quite different from the Guinness you've been drinking almost everywhere else in Ireland.

cork hostels
at a glance

HOSTEL	RATING	COST	IN A WORD	PAGE
Kinlay House		€11.50–€16.00	fancy	104
Sheila's		€13.00–€17.50	wonderful	104
Aran House Hostel		€10.50–€13.50	happy	101
Kelly's Hostel		€12.00–€20.00	good	102
Cork International		€12.50–€15.00	prim	102

aran house tourist hostel

Lower Glanmire Road, Cork, Co. Cork

Phone Number: 021–4551–566
Rates: €10.50–€13.50 per person (about $10.50–$13.50 US)
Beds: 25
Affiliation: IHO

This hostel is nice, small, and friendly enough to make even the wettest travelers feel welcome to Cork. They run a small half-kitchen, among other perks; hostellers we talked with liked the bunks, too.

Cleanliness:
Hospitality:
Party index:

how to get there:

By bus: Call hostel for transit route.
By car: Call hostel for directions.
By train: From Cork Station, walk next door to hostel.

cork international hostel

1-2 Redclyffe, Western Road, Cork, Co. Cork

Phone Number: 021–454–3289
Fax: 021–434–3715
E-mail: corkyh@gofree.indigo.ie
Rates: €12.50–€15.50 per HI member (about $13.00–$16.00 US)
Credit cards: Yes
Beds: 98
Private/family rooms: 18
Kitchen available: Yes
Office hours: Twenty-four hours
Affiliation: HI-AO
Extras: Meeting room, meals ($), bike rentals, shuttle ($), bureau de change, TV, store
Lockout: 10:30 A.M. to 1:30 P.M.

These renovated, sharp-looking Victorian brick town houses—we could swear we went to elementary school here, they look so prim—sit in a decent neighborhood with lotsa lively university students. But they're also fairly cramped and blah as hostels go. Too many beds are packed into the four floors of the place, and the kitchen needs work.

Insiders' tip:
Cork Museum is great

Party index:

Windows keep the sunlight coming in, but there are still better choices in town—although it's certainly safe and clean enough for your purposes if you're still coming this way. It's just not the peak experience it could be.

how to get there:

By bus: From bus station or Patricks Street, take 8 bus to hostel.
By car: Call hostel for directions.
By train: Cork Station is 1 mile away.

kelly's hostel

25 Summerhill South, Cork, Co. Cork

Phone Number: 021–4315–612
E-mail: kellyhostel@hotmail.com
Rates: €12–€20 (about $12–$20 US) per person
Beds: 20
Private/family rooms: 2
Affiliation: IHO, IHH
Extras: TV, laundry, lockers, bike rentals

Not much to report here yet—just a small, decent place with a literary bent and a fun common room. They maintain good facilities, too, with a laundry, lockers, and double rooms available—plus those unusual beasts, single rooms, for hostellers who just need to get away from all the rest of us for a night.

Best bet for a bite:
Quinnsworth Supermarket
Party index: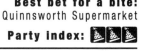

how to get there:

> **By bus:** Call hostel for transit route.
> **By car:** Call hostel for directions.
> **By train:** From Cork Station, call hostel for transit route.

key to icons

 Attractive natural setting

 Ecologically aware hostel

 Superior kitchen facilities or cafe

 Offbeat or eccentric place

 Superior bathroom facilities

 Romantic private rooms

 Comfortable beds

 A particularly good value

 Wheelchair accessible

 Good for business travelers

 Especially well suited for families

 Good for active travelers

 Visual arts at hostel or nearby

 Music at hostel or nearby

 Great hostel for skiers

 Bar or pub at hostel or nearby

 Editors' choice: among our very favorite hostels

kinlay house hostel

Bob & Joan's Walk, Shandon, Cork, Co. Cork

Phone Number: 021–4508–966
Fax: 021–4506–927
E-mail: kinlay.cork@usit.ie
Rates: €11.50–€16.00 per person (about $11.50–$16.00 US); doubles €40–€46 (about $40–$46 US)
Credit cards: Yes
Beds: 171
Private/family rooms: Yes
Affiliation: IHH
Extras: Bike rentals, breakfast, laundry, meals ($), pickups, bureau de change

A bit out of the way, this place is still another Cork winner anyway: clean, well-managed, rather fancy actually for a hostel. Every bed in the joint—the thirty-nine private rooms, the dorms, the single rooms—comes with free continental breakfast. That's not the only reason to stay, but it's a start. Staff respects your need to crash and/or mingle and provides opportunities for both. It's a little distant from downtown, but otherwise solid.

Best bet for a bite: On-site
Gestalt: Fun house
Hospitality:
Cleanliness:
Party index:

Don't forget to check out St. Ann Shandon next door, the beloved church with the huge weathervane. It's even possible (for a fee) to enter the place, hike seventeen stories to the tippy-top of the steeple, and ring the bells. Cool.

how to get there:

By bus: From Cork bus station, turn left on Merchant's Quay; make second right and cross Opera House bridge, then continue north on Upper Street.
By car: Call hostel for directions.
By train: From Cork Station, call hostel for directions.

sheila's cork tourist hostel

Belgrave Place, Wellington Road, Cork, Co. Cork

Phone Number: 021–4505–562
Fax: 021–4500–940
E-mail: info@sheilashostel.ie
Rates: €13.00–€17.50 per person (about $13.00–$17.50 US)
Credit cards: Yes
Beds: 158
Private/family rooms: Yes
Office hours: Twenty-four hours
Affiliation: IHH
Extras: Garden, breakfast ($), sauna, laundry, bureau de change, bike rentals, patio, coffee shop, VCR, TV, fireplace, e-mail, lockers, telegram office

Sheila's rules the roost in Cork City, that's all there is to say about it. Set aside your ideas about prim and proper hostels, and enjoy the show.

Housed in a funky building atop a hill, this hostel has views galore. Despite the panorama, though, you're very close to the central

Hospitality:
Party index:

downtown; only Isaac's is closer, and no other hostel in the city is close at all. You can sit out front and join a scene that appears ripped from the pages of, well, 1969, and still walk to town by lunchtime.

Inside the joint, it's great treatment all the way: Fresh scones grace the breakfast table. There's absolutely no lockout or curfew. You can send Western Union telegrams (i.e., requests to Mom and Dad for emergency $$$$) right from the hostel or exchange currency if you have some. There's a sauna. They'll even receive e-mail for you! Before you arrive! And you can use the computer in the lobby to send mail, too. Give us a break . . . it's too good.

Dorms are interestingly painted and fine; eighteen private rooms provide a chance to get away from the young hippoids who flock here. And the staff, well, let's just give 'em a capital A for awesome. They are heroic enough to locate open beds for you in case they're full.

Go see it, and tell us you don't agree. Sheila's is the top bunk in town.

how to get there:

By bus: From bus station, go right on Brian Boru Street, left on MacCurtain, right on York, and right onto Wellington.
By car: Call hostel for directions.
By train: Hostel is near Cork Station.

dingle town

Dingle gets our vote as one of the must-see little villages of Ireland. Located at the beginning of the beauteous Dingle Peninsula, it supplies all the music, beer, and good cheer you need. Heck, we're movin' here, it's so friendly. As an added bonus, the world-famous human-loving dolphin, Fungi, lives in a cove here—and can be swam right up to even to this day.

One drawback: In recent years, Americans (especially those who watch a certain chipper PBS travel icon) are discovering the place; that could mar the experience. Otherwise, Dingle's just dandy with us. The hostels are mostly good, too, with a notable exception or two.

To get here, take the train or bus to Tralee and then change to local buses—and mind the schedule, as the locals run only a half dozen or so times a day.

dingle hostels
at a glance

HOSTEL	RATING	COST	IN A WORD	PAGE
Ballintaggart House	◣	€12.50–€14.00	sporty	106
Rainbow Hostel	◣	€12.00–€14.00	rustic	108
Grapevine Hostel		€11.00–€13.00	central	107
Lovett's Hostel		€11.00	quiet	108

ballintaggart house hostel ◣

Racecourse Road, Dingle, Co. Kerry

Phone Number: 066–915–1454
Fax: 066–915–2207
E-mail: info@dingleaccommodation.com

Rates: €12.50–€14.00 per person (about $12.50–$14.00 US)
Credit cards: Yes
Beds: 118
Private/family rooms: Yes
Season: March 15 to October 31
Affiliation: IHH
Extras: Meals ($), breakfast, camping, laundry, bike rentals, pickups, shuttle, bureau de change, outings, horseback riding, fireplace, patio

Ah, another winning joint in Dingle. Thanks, IHH, this is what we needed: one of the best hostels in all Ireland.

Based in a former hunting lodge (but it's really more of a mansion) out on the edge of the cute little town, it's really good: horseback tours of the area, a gratis shuttle into town, free breakfast, and bike and wetsuit rentals

Hospitality:
Party index:

are all offered. (To swim up to Fungi the dolphin, silly.) The grand interior adds to the atmosphere, which improves considerably when you score a quad room instead of one of the bigger ten-bed dorms.

It's even rumored to be haunted—but the spirit, like Casper, is absolutely friendly. That's what they told us, anyway, and we believe 'em. You couldn't ask for nicer ownership than at this place.

Five private rooms and a cozy fire add to the individual and family fun.

how to get there:

By bus: Call hostel for transit route.
By car: Call hostel for directions.

grapevine hostel

Dyke Gate Lane, Dingle, Co. Kerry

Phone Number: 06691–51434
Rates: €11–€13 per person (about $11–$13 US); doubles €30 (about $30)
Private/family rooms: None
Kitchen available: Yes
Affiliation: None
Extras: Fireplace, stereo

Centrally located in hoppin' Dingle Town, this place is simply a coupla
beds—some with showers in the rooms—well placed for the pub-crawling action.

Hospitality:

Party Index:

Staff comes with a reputation for helpfulness, and they deliver; otherwise, it's just a simple bed.

how to get there:

By bus: From bus stop walk through Supervalue market. Turn right at front door and take first left. Continue walking down street to end. Hostel is on the left.

By car: Coming from Tralee/Killarney, turn right at roundabout, then first left and right again. Go past cinema and follow street to end.

lovett's hostel

Cooleen Road, Dingle, Co. Kerry

Phone Number: 06691–51903
Rates: €11 per person (about $11 US); doubles €30 (about $30 US)
Private/family rooms: Yes
Affiliation: None
Extras: Laundry

This isn't one of those places that's located right in cute Dingle Town;

Party Index:

it's a bit of a trek, but not terribly far. Nice views abound, and the place is decent enough.

Expect a tight fit, but hey—at least you'll get to meet fellow travelers up close and personal.

how to get there:

By bus: Call hostel for transit route.
By car: Call hostel for directions.

rainbow hostel

The Wood, Dingle, Co. Kerry

Phone Number: 06691–51044
Fax: 06691–52284
E-mail: rainbow@iol.ie
Beds: 20
Rates: €12–€14 per person (about $12–$14 US); doubles €28 (about $28 US)
Private/family rooms: Yes
Kitchen available: Yes
Affiliation: None
Extras: Camping, bike rentals, pickups, boat tours, barnyard animals, Internet access, laundry

Outside downtown Dingle but well done, this place is just about the town's top bunk. A farmhouse set in the pleasant outskirts (it's roughly a mile or so), the Rainbow features great management that actually tries helping hostellers enjoy themselves for a change. You never know who'll show up here, and for once that's a good thing.

They'll give you a lift from the town's bus stop, run boat trips around the gorgeous Dingle Peninsula to see famous dolphins and other sea creatures, even rent you a bike. The kitchen

Gestalt: Pot o' gold
Hospitality:
Party Index:

really makes use of its space well. Cool decor, too. Yet another bonus: This hostel is at the beginning of the wondrously scenic Slea Head Loop, which isn't as well known as some loops in these parts.

Note: Don't confuse this place with the Rainbow Hostel in Doolin. Both are nice, but still . . .

how to get there:

By bus: Call hostel for transit route.
By car: Call hostel for directions.

shiplake mountain hostel

Shiplake, Dunmanway, Co. Cork

Phone Number: 023–45750
Fax: 023–45750
Rates: €11 per person (about $11 US); doubles €25–€36 (about $25–$36 US)
Beds: 20
Private/family rooms: Yes

Shiplake Mountain Hostel
Dunmanway, Co. Cork
(Photo courtesy of Shiplake Mountain Hostel)

Kitchen available: Yes
Affiliation: IHH
Extras: Meals ($), camping, laundry, bike rentals, cycling trips, woodstove, store, pickups

This great hostel—one of Ireland's best, in scenic west Cork County—is also pretty unusual, featuring such touches as cool gypsy caravans for private rooms, a great outdoorsy setting, and delicious veggie-only meals. Think crunchy granola city, but it tastes good! The nice private room, a camping area, occasional cycling outings, and a range of ad hoc classes make it even more fun.

But back to those caravans in the garden. They're "barrel-top,"

Gestalt: Shipshape
Hospitality:
Cleanliness:
Party index:

meaning they resemble huge, brightly colored barrels with the tops cut off. You (two to four of you) sleep inside the contraption, using electric light and heating to make yourself more comfortable. Besides the caravans, they've got two dorm rooms—one with eight beds and one containing six. In a strange twist, they require sleeping bags here rather than ban them.

Just remember that the hostel is almost 3 miles outside Dunmanway. (Of course, hostel staff will sometimes pick you up if you call 'em and shuttle you into town for occasional pub nights.) All in all, a good and efficiently run place. It's just too bad they've got only twenty beds here. Once the word spreads about this place, you could easily find yourself shut out from a bed—and that would be a shame.

how to get there:

By bus: From Cork, take Bus Éireann to Dunmanway and call hostel for pickup.

By car: From Dunmanway, take Castel Road from town 2½ miles toward Kealkill; turn right at hostel sign.

By train: From Cork Station, take Bus Éireann to Dunmanway and call hostel for pickup.

dunquin hostel

Dunquin, Ballyferriter, Tralee, Co. Kerry

Phone Number: 066–915–6121
Fax: 066–915–6355
Rates: €10.00–€13.00 per HI member (about $10.00–$13.00 US)
Credit cards: None
Beds: 52
Private/family rooms: Yes
Kitchen available: Yes
Office hours: 7:00 to 10:00 A.M.; 5:00 P.M. to midnight
Affiliation: HI-AO
Extras: Store, meals ($)

Right near the Blasket Islands ferry, this town and hostel have the nearby Atlantic for a neighbor. Next stop, North America.

This place is actually quite plain, just two white buildings in a mostly treeless landscape. It's merely adequate as a base for explorations of the interesting views and archaeology. If you don't dig the six-, eight-, or ten-bed dorms, pay extra if you want

Gestalt: Blasket ball
Cleanliness:
Party index:

access to double or quad rooms, which slightly improve the comfort level. A few foodstuffs are also sold here. Don't expect luxury.

They once built an entire village here for an American movie (it figures), and parts of the set still stand. But never mind that. The local pubs are where the real fun is, as well as a burgeoning arts and crafts scene way out here on Slea Head. Painters and craft artists particularly love it. Also don't miss the Blasket Centre, which explains those rocky, grassy (though hostel-free) islets just offshore.

how to get there:

By bus: In summer, take Bus Éireann from Killarney to Dún Chaoin and get off at hostel. In winter, from Dingle take Bus Eireann connection to Dún Chaoin.

By car: Call hostel for directions.

By train: Contact hostel for transit route.

murphy's village hostel

The Village, Glengarriff, Co. Cork

Phone Number: 027–63555
Fax: 027–63555
E-mail: murphyshostel@eircom.net
Rates: €12–€15 per person (about $12–$15 US); doubles €32 (about $32 US)
Credit cards: None
Beds: 33
Private/family rooms: Yes
Office hours: Vary, usually open
Affiliation: IHH
Extras: Laundry, kitchen, breakfast, Internet access, meals ($)

Gestalt:
Village people

Insiders' tip:
Blue Loo for music

Hospitality:

Cleanliness:

Party index:

This fairly new place looks good to us, with good banana muffins for breakfast, a restaurant on premises, and Internet access, too. The welcome couldn't be warmer.

The area's great for sea kayaking, biking (get one in the village, not at the hostel), or hiking. Hardbodies might want to scale Hungry Hill, and the rest of us can explore Glengarriff National Forest.

how to get there:

By bus: Contact hostel for transit details.
By car: Contact hostel for directions.
By train: Contact hostel for transit details.

failte hostel

Shelbourne Street, Kenmare, Co. Kerry

Phone Number: 064–42333
Fax: 066–42466
E-mail: failtefinn@eircom.net
Rates: €12 per person (about $12 US); doubles €32–€40 (about $32–$40 US)
Beds: 39
Private/family rooms: Yes
Season: April 1 to October 31
Affiliation: IHH
Extras: Bike rentals, courtyard, TV, VCR, terrace, stove, taxi
Curfew: 1:00 A.M.

Make sure you find the right hostel here; you could get confused. This is the really nice three-tiered building across from the town post office—obviously some wealthy person's house that was turned into lodgings for us slackers.

Just kiddin'. Anyhow, medium-sized dorm rooms were clean and roomy enough for us; two private rooms are also charming. The courtyard and cool camping area were other bonuses.

Insiders' tip:
Big stone circle in town

Gestalt: Ken-do
Hospitality:
Party index:

There's not a whole heckuva lot to do in Kenmare proper, but the surrounding countryside is really nice.

how to get there:

By bus: Call hostel for transit route.
By car: Call hostel for directions.

killarney

The most scenic town in Ireland? Yup, without a doubt. And ya know what? Everyone and their brother knows it, too.

Ah, Killarney. If you can stand hordes of horse-drawn tourists, come by all means; this is a handsome setting indeed. But we'd rather stick to the park and the outskirts, where the trees can occasionally be glimpsed through the packs of tour buses.

Hostels here tend to be just fair to middling, unlike in most other Irish cities; we guess that it's because people will pay anything to sleep here. And so they do. Let the buyer beware.

killarney hostels
at a glance

HOSTEL	RATING	COST	IN A WORD	PAGE
Ring of Kerry House	◣	€11.00–€17.00	popular	118
Neptune's Hostel	◣	€11.00–€16.00	helpful	116
Killarney Railway Hostel	◣	€11.50–€17.50	comfortable	115
Peacock Farm Hostel	◣	€10.00–€12.00	rural	117
Súgán Hostel		€12.00–€14.00	tasty	119
Park Hostel		€10.00	unknown	117
Fossa Holiday Hostel		€10.00–€11.00	plain	114

fossa holiday hostel
Fossa, Killarney, Co. Kerry

Phone Number: 064–31497

Fax: 064–34459
E-mail: fossaholidays@eircom.net
Rates: €10–€11 per person (about $10–$11 US)
Credit cards: Yes
Beds: 40
Private/family rooms: No
Season: April 4 to September 30
Affiliation: IHH
Extras: Meals ($), laundry, bike rentals, camping, tennis courts

Located a bit outside of town, this used to be mostly a campsite. Now there's some hostel accommoda-   **Party index:** 🎉🎉

tions, forty beds in plain dorms. It's certainly cheap, but that's about all we can say about it. Not a top pick by any means.

how to get there:

By bus: Call hostel for transit route.
By car: Call hostel for directions.
By train: Call hostel for transit route.

killarney railway hostel

Fair Hill, Killarney, Co. Kerry

Phone Number: 064–35299
Fax: 064–32197
Rates: €11.50–€17.50 per person (about $11.50–$17.50 US); doubles €35 (about $35 US)
Beds: 101
Private/family rooms: Yes
Affiliation: IHH
Extras: Laundry, camping, meals ($), bike rentals, pool table

Despite its location near Killarney's rail station, this place is actually pretty nice and comfortable—and big enough to handle the hosteller load, too. That's a switch from the usual transit-district flophouses.

Gestalt: Train a comin'
Party index: 🎉🎉🎉

Dorms range in size anywhere from quads to ten or twelve beds per room. The recent fix ups have helped, too, and twelve private rooms add further comfort to the mix.

how to get there:

By bus: Bus station in Killarney; call hostel for pickup.
By car: Call hostel for directions.
By train: Train station in Killarney; call hostel for pickup.

neptune's town hostel

New Street, Killarney, Co. Kerry

Phone Number: 064–35255
Fax: 064–36399
E-mail: neptune@eircom.net
Rates: €11–€16 per person (about $11–$16 US); doubles €32–€40 (about $32–$40 US)
Credit cards: Yes
Beds: 137
Private/family rooms: Yes
Affiliation: IHH
Extras: Meals ($), laundry, bike rental, bureau de change, tour discounts, lockers, Internet

Good dorm rooms come six to ten beds a pop at this nice downtown Killarney hostel, although the specialty appears to be the eight private rooms—almost as good as rooms at an inn, but at just a fraction of the cost.

Hospitality:
Cleanliness:
Party index:

Lots of tourism information is available at the front desk, and you can book tours there, too, sometimes at a hosteller discount. It's big enough to handle the masses of tourist hostellers pouring into town each summer, so you're a little less likely to get shut out of a bed than at smaller, cozier places.

Tons of other services, like a currency exchange, free lockers, plentiful kitchen, and bike rentals, help make this a good choice as well. The only drawback is the common area, which feels lifeless.

how to get there:

By bus: Call hostel for transit route.
By car: Call hostel for directions.
By train: Train station in Killarney; call hostel for transit route.

park hostel

Park Road, Killarney, Co. Kerry

Phone Number: 064–32119
Rates: €10 per person (about $10 US); doubles €20 (about $20 US)
Beds: 50
Private/family rooms: Yes
Season: April 1 to November 1
Affiliation: IHH
Extras: Laundry, camping

This place, set a bit outside downtown near a gas station, is rather simple and uninspiring. It contains one private room, a ton of bunk beds, plus an attached camping area and a working laundry.

Party index:

If you want to get out of Killarney and experience a bit of nature, as well as meet some folks from around Europe, this might be a possibility. Otherwise, we'd stay at one of the other excellent places in town instead.

how to get there:

By bus: Call hostel for transit route.
By car: From Cork Road, turn onto Park Road; hostel is across from gas station.
By train: Train station in Killarney; call hostel for transit route.

peacock farm hostel

Gortdromkiery, Muckross, Killarney, Co. Kerry

Phone Number: 064–33557
E-mail: peacockhostel@eircom.net
Rates: €10–€12 per person (about $10–$12 US); doubles €28 (about $28 US)
Beds: 20

Private/family rooms: Yes
Season: April 1 to September 30
Affiliation: IHH
Extras: Pickups, laundry

It's way outside Killarney—a good 5 or 6 miles, by the look of it—but the helpful owners will sometimes pick you

Gestalt: Cocky
Hospitality: 🖐
Party index: 🎉

up in the big town if you call ahead. The location's a stunner: It's right on a lake, and there are peacocks on the property.

As a hostel, it's smallish but friendly, and obviously quite rural; the price here (which includes sheets) is more than fair for such a nice taste of country life. The dorms are fine and have a nice homey feel to them. One private room is also kept open for couples, as a bonus. Other amenities include a laundry.

While you're here, get over to Muckross Abbey, a fourteenth-century monastery that's quintessentially Irish. Other interesting places nearby are Lough Leane (Lower Lake) and Muckross Lake (Middle Lake).

how to get there:

By bus: Bus station in Killarney; call hostel for pickup.
By car: Call hostel for directions.
By train: Train station in Killarney; call hostel for pickup

ring of kerry hostel 🖐

Killarney, Co. Kerry

Phone Number: 064–31240
Fax: 064–34300
E-mail: anoige@killarney.iol.ie
Rates: €11–€17 per HI member (about $11–$17 US)
Credit cards: Yes
Beds: 186
Private/family rooms: 7
Kitchen available: Yes
Office hours: Twenty-four hours
Affiliation: HI-AO

Extras: Bike rentals, meals ($), meeting room, laundry, pickups, tours, Internet, bureau de change, TV

Friendlier and groovier than many of Europe's other HI-affiliated joints, this slightly scary looking seventeenth-century mansion of stone a couple miles outside central Killarney makes up for its bigness with decent treatment. Heck, they'll even pick you up sometime from the train or bus station, and that's awfully nice of them. (Competition will do that to ya.)

And how 'bout that location? We're talking seventy-five acres of woods and lawns, plus a view of both lakes and mountains. At last, a chance to get away from the choking Killarney

crowds for a few hours. Now this is why we came to Ireland in the first place.

But with success comes a price: It's essential to book ahead in summertime, as this place gets jammed in a hurry. Schoolkids are especially fond of the hostel, as schools enjoy booking hordes of their kiddies in for summertime outings. So pay more for a double or quad room, if you can get one, to avoid the crush in the six- and eight-bed dorms. At night, amuse yourself watching rabbits carpet the hostel lawn, and plan on taking one of the hostel-sponsored day tours of the area's gorgeous scenery.

Just don't expect to do it all alone.

how to get there:

By bus: Killarney bus station is 3 miles; call hostel for pickup.

By car: Hostel is 3 miles west of downtown Killarney; call for directions.

By train: Killarney Station is 3 miles; call hostel for pickup.

súgán hostel

Lewis Road, Killarney, Co. Kerry

Phone Number: 064–33104
Fax: 064–32578
Rates: €12–€14 per person (about $12–$14 US)

Beds: 18
Private/family rooms: None
Affiliation: IHO
Extras: Meals ($), fireplace, bike rentals

A small two-story stone cottage close to Killarney Station, the Súgán is famous for one reason and one only: the food, mate.

The whole-foods meals at the restaurant beneath this hostel aren't

Gestalt: Súgán, Súgán
Hospitality:
Party Index:

always cheap, but, man, are they delicious! You might end up eating here even if you get shut out of a room—and that's a real possibility, as there are just eighteen beds wedged into rooms too small for their good. (There aren't enough bathrooms, either. Only one showerhead for the whole deal? Yikes.)

Sadly, there's no kitchen either—almost unforgiveable—but you will get a discount at the terrific Súgán Kitchen at least. We'd eat there and sleep elsewhere, given a choice. If you do end up sleeping here, though, it isn't too bad to hang out in the common room, which possesses its own especially mellow vibe.

key to icons

 Attractive natural setting

 Ecologically aware hostel

 Superior kitchen facilities or cafe

 Offbeat or eccentric place

 Superior bathroom facilities

 Romantic private rooms

 Comfortable beds

 A particularly good value

 Wheelchair accessible

 Good for business travelers

 Especially well suited for families

 Good for active travelers

 Visual arts at hostel or nearby

 Music at hostel or nearby

Great hostel for skiers

Bar or pub at hostel or nearby

Editors' choice: among our very favorite hostels

how to get there:

By bus: From bus station, walk left on Park Road, then right on Lewis.

By car: Call hostel for directions.

By train: From Killarney Station, walk left on Park Road, then right on Lewis.

laune valley farm hostel

Banshagh, Killorglin, Co. Kerry

Phone Number: 066–976–1488
Fax: 066–976–1488
Rates: €13–€14 per person (about $13–$14 US); doubles €34–€40 (about $34–$40 US)
Beds: 25
Private/family rooms: 4
Affiliation: IHH, IHO
Extras: Meals ($), TV, camping, laundry, store

We can't believe how many of these good Irish hostels are attached to farms. And this is another: real hospitality in the real countryside. Pinch us! We never knew hostels could be this good.

This place is out in the countryside (you knew that from the name, right?) and features a campground, laundry, twenty-five beds, and four private rooms—plus the sounds and smells of the farmyard animals for free. You can buy eggs and other stuff from the owners on site. There's also a television, for some reason, but the owners partially atone for that by serving good meals here.

Gestalt: Laune party
Hospitality:
Party index:

This is a genuine Irish town, not a tourist trap, so local excitement consists of hitting a pub or restaurant after an afternoon of checking out the local castle ruins.

how to get there:

By bus: Call hostel for transit route.
By car: Call hostel for directions.
By train: Call hostel for transit route.

dempsey's hostel

Eastern Road, Kinsale, Co. Cork

Phone Number: 021–4772–124
Rates: €10 per person (about $10 US); doubles €20 (about $20 US)
Credit cards: Yes
Beds: 32
Private/family rooms: Yes
Affiliation: IHH
Extras: Camping

This pretty simple hostel is located near downtown Kinsale, a town known through Ireland as one with really great food. Most of those seafood restaurants are probably out of your financial reach, however. So satisfy yourself instead by poking around the ruins of the old walls and battlements that once enclosed and protected the town from attacking boats.

Best bet for a bite: U-pick

Party index: 🍸

The joint itself is okay, with a campground and seven private rooms in addition to the usual bunks. They charge you for showers, for some reason; sure, hot water costs, but give us a break.

As far as other attractions go, there aren't a whole lot to pick from. Desmond Castle is one, though: The place was built around 1500 as a Spanish and then a French castle and prison. Now it houses something far cooler, the International Museum of Wine.

If you're looking for a bike trip, hit Charles Fort, built out on a peninsula just outside town. The fort's shaped like a star and was originally constructed to keep nasty invaders out of Kinsale. You can get a tour from spring until fall, though it'll cost you a little bit of cash.

how to get there:

By bus: Call hostel for transit route.
By car: Call hostel for directions.
By train: Call hostel for transit route.

glanmore lake hostel

Glanmore Lake, Lauragh, Killarney, Co. Kerry

Phone Number: 064–83181
Rates: €10–€13 per HI member (about $10–$13 US)
Credit cards: None
Beds: 36
Private/family rooms: None
Kitchen available: Yes
Office hours: 7:00 to 10:00 A.M.; 5:00 P.M. to midnight
Season: March 28 to May 30, weekends only; June 1 to September 30, daily
Affiliation: HI-AO
Extras: Meeting room
Curfew: 11:30 P.M.

A cute, almost Alpine-looking schoolhouse located at the foot of spectacular Tim Healy Pass contains this hostel, which is also fronted by a handy lake. Couldn't do much better than that for location. (This region of Ireland is as wild as they come—mountains, lakes, the sea, woods; it's all here.)

Hospitality:
Cleanliness:
Party index:

And the hostel, as befits the supreme location, is surprisingly laid-back for an An Oige joint. There are four rooms, with eight to ten bunks each. The mild, sea-tempered climate around here will astound you—or, if it's raining for days, drive you nuts.

how to get there:

By bus: From Killarney, take Bus Éireann (summer only) toward Castletownbere to Lauragh; walk 4 miles to hostel. From Cork (summer only), take bus to Ardgroom, 8 miles away.

By car: Follow R572 from Glengarriff and make right at Adrigole. From Kenmare, take R571 and turn left at Lauragh.

By train: Killarney Station, 35 miles away, is the nearest stop.

an stor midleton tourist hostel

Drury's Avenue, Midleton, Co. Cork

Phone Number: 021–4633–106

Fax: 021–4631–399
E-mail: anstor@eircom.net
Rates: €12.50–€13.50 per person (about $12.50–$13.50 US); doubles €35–€37 (about $35–$37 US)
Credit cards: Yes
Beds: 30
Private/family rooms: Yes
Affiliation: IHH
Extras: Laundry, bike rentals

This converted mill, just 10 miles east of Cork city, is really good.

Hospitality:
Cleanliness:
Party index:

There's one private room, a mess of bunks, a laundry, and some bikes for rent. Rooms all have en-suite bathrooms, which is nice for a change. Everything is kept clean and trim, and the staff does a good job of making it all a fun experience.

While here, don't miss a tour of the local Jameson Irish whiskey distillery—and, of course, a taste.

how to get there:

By bus: Call hostel for transit route.
By car: Call hostel for directions.
By train: Call hostel for transit route.

schull backpackers lodge

Colla Road, Schull, Co. Cork

Phone Number: 028–28681
Fax: 028–27037
Rates: €11.50–€12.00 per person (about $12.00 US); doubles €33–€40 (about $33–$40 US)
Credit cards: Yes
Beds: 31
Private/family rooms: Yes
Affiliation: IHH
Extras: Laundry, bike rentals, camping

Tucked in a rural setting a short distance from little Schull's little harbor, this newish and friendly place reminds us—yet again—why southwest Ireland is so great. And so are the hostels.

Snag one of three private rooms for maximum comfort; otherwise, doze in the nice dorms and make sure to check out the close-by pub scene.

The Mizen Head Peninsula is nowhere near as busy as Killarney, the views are stupendous, and Schull's (that's "skull's") profusion of pubs and grub makes this joint by far the liveliest base in the area.

Insiders' tip:
Foreshore walk along coast

Gestalt: Schull cap

Hospitality:

Party index:

how to get there:

By bus: Call hostel for transit route.
By car: Call hostel for directions.

russagh mill hostel

Castletownshend Road, Skibbereen, Co. Cork

Phone Number: 028–22451
Fax: 028–21256
Rates: €11–€12 per person (about $11–$12 US); doubles €30–€34 (about $30–$34 US)
Beds: 50
Private/family rooms: Yes
Season: April 16 to October 30
Affiliation: IHH
Extras: Camping, bike rentals, tours, outings

This is one of Ireland's very best hostels if you're an outdoors type, especially since the active owner opened an "adventure center" right on the premises. It really is a mill, centuries old, about a mile from the town.

You can sign up for sailboarding or canoeing trips here, or you can hike and bike around the area. The hostel also has a campground and eight private rooms. The crowd? Well, let's just put it this way. Rules and lockouts definitely won't be a problem at this place.

Expect to meet lots of Americans and Euros in this part of the country; the pretty scenery and formerly cheap land (foreigners can't buy Irish soil anymore) lured them here during the '70s and '80s, and here they remain today.

Best bet for a bite: Friday market

Gestalt: Thanks, a mill

Party index:

Nearby Lough Hyne (that's Lake Hyne to you and me) is a possible side trip; it's a saltwater lake connected to the sea by rapids and has been designated as a nature reserve.

how to get there:

By bus: Call hostel for transit route.
By car: Call hostel for directions.
By train: Call hostel for transit route.

---

harbour view hostel

Kenmare Road, Sneem, Co. Kerry

Phone Number: 064–45276
Rates: €10–€14 per person (about $10–$14 US); doubles €44 (about $44 US)
Beds: 24
Private/family rooms: Yes
Affiliation: None
Extras: Campground, meals ($), laundry, camping, free pickups, bike rentals

Located on the Ring of Kerry, Sneem isn't exactly a thriving metropolis—but it is one of southwestern Ireland's most colorful towns, with pastel-colored houses brightening up an otherwise plain main street.

The hostel here isn't super, either. Plain rooms and no view are the rule, although an attached campground provides a brief opportunity to pretend you're roughing it in Ireland's actual beauty.

An interesting diversion if you're here, though, is the sculpture park referred to by locals as "The Pyramids." It will become obvious why once you see it; some of the sculptures were loosely based on the ancient beehive-shaped stone structures so common around this part of Ireland.

Party index:

how to get there:

By bus: Call hostel for transit route.
By car: Call hostel for directions.
By train: Call hostel for transit route.

conor pass hostel

Stradbally, Castlegregory, Co. Kerry

Phone Number: 066–713–9179
Fax: 066–713–9533
Rates: €13 per person (about $13 US); doubles €26 (about $26 US)
Credit cards: Yes
Beds: 8
Private/family rooms: Yes
Season: March 15 to October 31
Affiliation: IHH
Extras: Meals ($)

A homey place—because it's in a house—this place shouldn't be full when you roll in, despite its small size (just eight beds). Nice dorms, although there aren't a lot of extras here with your bed: It's merely a kindly place to sleep, which is sometimes all you need. It does have the usual kitchen and common area, too, and they serve meals for a charge.

Insiders' tip:
Steam engine museum

Hospitality:
Party index:

Stradbally? It's a one-horse (actually, one-street) town. If you're dying to see something interesting—and you could well be after a night here—Emo Court, a blockish eighteenth-century building with extensive grounds, sits nearby. Hiking is also popular in the mountains that overlook the town.

how to get there:

By bus: Call hostel for transit route.
By car: Call hostel for directions.
By train: Call hostel for transit route.

ferry house hostel

The Square, Tarbert, Co. Kerry

Phone Number: 068–36555
Fax: 068–36555
Rates: €10 (about $10 US); doubles €34–€40 (about $34–$40 US)
Beds: 36
Affiliation: IHH
Extras: Meals ($), camping, laundry, bike rentals, pickups

Pretty new and smack in the heart of little Tarbert, this is a good option when you're heading over to County Clare and need a bunk for the night. The hostel's pretty, in a fading, Old World kinda way. This was once a nice hotel, and it still retains traces of glory: Four of the rooms are still used as doubles. They've stocked the place with a hosteller laundry, a small snack shop, and a campground on site. The staff will also do pickups if you need 'em and rent you a bike if you need that.

Insiders' tip: Use the ferry!
Gestalt: Ferry good
Hospitality:
Party index:

key to icons

 Attractive natural setting

 Ecologically aware hostel

 Superior kitchen facilities or cafe

 Offbeat or eccentric place

 Superior bathroom facilities

 Romantic private rooms

 Comfortable beds

 A particularly good value

 Wheelchair accessible

 Good for business travelers

Especially well suited for families

 Good for active travelers

 Visual arts at hostel or nearby

 Music at hostel or nearby

Great hostel for skiers

 Bar or pub at hostel or nearby

 Editors' choice: among our very favorite hostels

how to get there:
By bus: Call hostel for transit route.
By car: Call hostel for directions.
By train: Call hostel for transit route.

tralee

The only town of any size on the Dingle Peninsula, this is far from the interesting parts but a necessary pass-through point: It's the end point for trains and the starting point for buses running around the peninsula. A bit bland, sure, but a good place to stock up before experiencing the wonders of Dingle.

Hostels here aren't bad at all—in fact, you really can't go wrong here.

tralee hostels
at a glance

HOSTEL	RATING	COST	IN A WORD	PAGE
Collis-Sandes Hostel	◤	€11.50–€16.00	handsome	129
Lisnagree Hostel	◤	€13.00	homey	131
Westward Court Hostel		€15.00–€17.00	newish	132
Courthouse Lodge Hostel		€14.00–€17.00	okay	130

collis-sandes hostel ◤

Oakpark, Tralee, Co. Kerry

Phone Number: 066–712–8658
Fax: 066–712–8658
E-mail: colsands@indigo.ie

Rates: €11.50–€16.00 per person (about $11.50–$16.00 US); €24–€44
(about $24–$44 US)
Credit cards: Yes
Beds: 84
Private/family rooms: 9
Season: June 1 to September 30
Affiliation: IHH
Extras: Pickups, laundry, camping, garden

Attention to detail makes this Georgian estate-turned-hostel a real
winner, the best bed in town probably. Too bad it's some distance from
being central.

But the dorm rooms are in good shape and well lighted to boot, plus
there are nine sort-of-private rooms available for couples. Obviously
the interior's a lot nicer than you've come to expect a hostel's to be, with
all sorts of little architectural flourishes to remind you that rich people
once lived here.

The hostel grounds and free lifts from the bus and train stations are
welcome touches indeed.

Best bet for a bite:
Vegetarian place in town

Hospitality:

Cleanliness:

Party index:

Not exactly in downtown Tralee, as we said, so you're a bit of a distance from food and nightlife without a car.

how to get there:

By bus: From bus station, call hostel for free pickup.
By car: Call hostel for directions.
By train: From Tralee Station, call hostel for free pickup.

courthouse lodge hostel

5 Church Street, Tralee, Co. Kerry

Phone Number: 066-712-719
Fax: 066–712–7199
Rates: €9.00–€10.00 per person (about $9.00–$10.00 US); doubles
€25–€30 (about $25–$30 US)
Beds: 30
Private/family rooms: Yes

Kitchen available: Yes
Affiliation: IHH
Extras: TV lounge, VCR, laundry, Internet access ($), meals

Right in the action—not that there's all that much "action" in Tralee—this hostel delivers decent bunks, and all rooms have en-suite bathrooms. The shared televison lounge

Party index: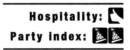

(with video playing potential), communal kitchen, and laundry enhance the feel of the place.

Nobody around, nothing going on in town? Log on via the hostel's Internet terminal and write e-mails home about how great Tralee is.

how to get there:

By bus: From bus station, walk 100 yards west on North Circular to Ashe Street; turn left and continue less than 100 yards to Church Street; turn right and continue to hostel on left.

By car: Contact hostel for directions.

By train: From Tralee station, walk 100 yards west on North Circular to Ashe Street; turn left and continue less than 100 yards to Church Street; turn right and continue to hostel on left.

lisnagree hostel

Ballinorig Road, Tralee, Co. Kerry

Phone Number: 066–712–7133
Rates: €13 per person (about $13 US); doubles €36 (about $36 US)
Beds: 20
Private/family rooms: 5
Kitchen available: Yes
Affiliation: IHH
Extras: Bureau de change, tours

This is yet another good hostel in Tralee, the landlocked jumping-off point for the marvelous Dingle Peninsula.

The hostel is small but homey, con-

Hospitality:
Party index: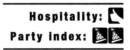

sisting of just twenty beds plus five private rooms for couples or families. Definitely the pick of the litter in town for private rooms. Facilities such as the kitchen are also nicely maintained.

how to get there:

By bus: Call hostel for transit route.
By car: Call hostel for directions.
By train: Call hostel for transit route.

westward court hostel

Mary Street, Tralee, Co. Kerry

Phone Number: 066–718–0081
Fax: 066–718–0082
E-mail: westward@iol.ie
Rates: €15–€17 per person (about $15–$17 US); doubles €44–€52 (about $44–$52 US)
Credit cards: None
Beds: 85
Private/family rooms: Yes
Affiliation: IHH
Extras: Breakfast, laundry, bike rentals

Gestalt: Westward home
Party index: 🍕🍕

This hostel appears to be a good place for families and couples—management is reporting a full twenty-five double rooms among its total of eighty-five beds.

Other amenities include a laundry, free breakfast, and bikes for hire.

how to get there:

By bus: Contact hostel for transit route.
By car: Contact hostel for directions.
By train: Contact hostel for transit route.

maria's schoolhouse hostel

Cahergal, Union Hall, Co. Cork

Phone Number: 028–33002
Fax: 028–33002
E-mail: mariasschoolhouse@eircom.net
Rates: €12 per person (about $12 US); doubles €46–€50 (about $46–$50 US)
Credit cards: Yes
Beds: 32
Private/family rooms: 9
Affiliation: IHH
Extras: Laundry, meals ($), pickups, bike rentals, fireplace, outings, canoe lessons

You couldn't ask for much more in a hostel, especially one that used to be just a functional schoolhouse. Now there's an open fireplace, a laundry, meatless and nonmeatless meals, great beds, and bike rentals. Nine private rooms are an additional bonus, as is the legendary hospitality here.

Insiders' tip: Connolly's bar for great music

Gestalt: Ave Maria

Hospitality:

Party index:

Don't miss the outings, planned by the same staff in swashbuckling fashion.

how to get there:

By bus: Call hostel for pickup.
By car: Call hostel for directions.
By train: Call hostel for transit route.

ring lyne hostel

Chapeltown, Valentia Island, Co. Kerry

Phone Number: 066–9476103
Fax: 066–9476174
Rates: €10–€15 per person (about $10–$15 US)
Beds: 12

Private/family rooms: 3
Affiliation: IHO
Extras: Breakfast, laundry, bike rentals, meals ($), pub

So what's the story, morning glory? Teeny Valentia Island has not one, not two, but three working hostels . . . possibly the highest per-capita hostel ratio in the world.

All three suffice, but this one—brought to you by the folks at IHO—is as good as any other, if fairly plain. Its dorms and common areas display thoughtfulness, and the private rooms with breakfast included are worth the extra cost.

Insiders' tip:
Ogham stones around island

Party index:

This is some location, too, close to the island's natural wonders but also near pubs and takeout stands.

Don't overlook the in-hostel restaurant or bar, either, which serves your typical surf and turf type entrees along with beer and wine.

how to get there:

By bus: Call hostel for transit route.

By car: Cross bridge onto island and continue 2 miles to Chapeltown; hostel is central in town.

key to icons

 Attractive natural setting

 Comfortable beds

 Good for active travelers

 Ecologically aware hostel

 A particularly good value

 Visual arts at hostel or nearby

 Superior kitchen facilities or cafe

 Wheelchair accessible

Music at hostel or nearby

Offbeat or eccentric place

Good for business travelers

Great hostel for skiers

 Superior bathroom facilities

 Especially well suited for families

Bar or pub at hostel or nearby

Romantic private rooms

Editors' choice: among our very favorite hostels

By ferry: From Knightstown ferry (operates summertime only), go 3 miles to Chapeltown; hostel is central in town.

royal pier hostel

Knightstown, Valentia Island, Co. Kerry

Phone Number: 066–9476144
Fax: 066–9476186
E-mail: royalpier-val@ireland.com
Rates: €15–€20 per person (about $15–$20 US)
Beds: 35
Private/family rooms: Yes
Affiliation: IHO
Extras: Restaurant ($), tours, laundry

This big house looks imposing but is actually pretty small: only thirty-five beds to fight for. Hostellers report that the private room is the nicest of the bunch.

Complaints? Yeah, a few. It's not the friendliest place and not the comfiest either. Tsk, tsk. Still, the on-site restaurant is adequate in a pinch, and hostel staff sometimes hook you up with tours of the area.

Gestalt: Pier 1
Hospitality:
Party index:

how to get there:

By bus: Call hostel for transit route.
By car: Call hostel for directions.
By train: Call hostel for transit route.

valentia island hostel

Knightstown, Valentia Island, Co. Kerry

Phone Number: 066–947–6154
Rates: €10.50–€13.00 per person (about $10.50–$13.00 US)
Credit cards: None

Beds: 40
Private/family rooms: Yes
Office hours: 7:00 to 10:30 A.M.; 5:00 P.M. to midnight
Season: June 1 to September 30
Affiliation: HI-AO

Formerly three cottages of a coast guard station, this joint is probably the most basic of the island's trio of hostels. Still, it offers great views

Party index:

of the island harbor. The island is actually reached by car or bike over a bridge. Once here, rooms contain two to ten beds each; families will enjoy the four smaller rooms.

Valentia's main natural draw is its tropical gardens, possible because of the mild Gulf Stream–bred winds that touch Ireland here. Check 'em out.

how to get there:

By bus: From Killarney, take Bus Éireann toward Cahersiveen to Reenard Point; take ferry to Valentia Island, turn right, and walk 1 mile to hostel.
By car: Call hostel for directions.
By train: Nearest train station is in Killarney, 43 miles away.

peter's place hostel

Waterville, Co. Kerry

Phone Number: 066–947–4608
Rates: €10 per person (about $10 US); doubles €25 (about $25 US)
Beds: 12
Private/family rooms: 2
Affiliation: None
Extras: Meals (sometimes), camping, fireplace, laundry

Insiders' tip:
Standing stones nearby

Gestalt: Peter principle

Hospitality: 🔦

Party index: 🎉🎉🎉

Just a town house, and as casual as casual could be. There aren't many beds here, so you have to weigh that against the perks of being in a small place. Meals are sometimes served, sometimes not . . . we couldn't really figure out when. Sheets are included with overnight rate.

There's an attached campground and good-smelling fire, too, and the owner is cool. So give it a look.

how to get there:

By bus: Call hostel for transit route.
By car: Call hostel for directions.

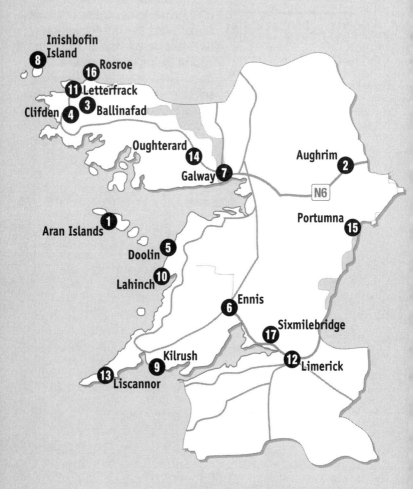

western ireland

Western Ireland takes a close second to the southwest as the drop-dead most scenic part of the country. (Who decides these things, anyway?)

Galway is the obvious big-town stop, a place whose reputation grows annually as a junction of Irish tradition and slightly cosmopolitan culture. But there are plenty of other spots to hit, including little Clifden for instance; if you can stand the more monotonous food of the small towns, you'll be rewarded by real conversations and more and more of that famous Irish landscape.

bru radharc na mara hostel

Inishere Island, Aran Islands, Co. Galway

Phone Number: 099–75024
Fax: 099–75024
E-mail: maire.searraigh@oceanfree.net
Rates: €12 per person (about $12 US); doubles: €32 (about $32 US)
Credit cards: Yes
Beds: 39
Private/family rooms: 2
Season: March 1 to October 31
Affiliation: IHH
Extras: Laundry, meals ($), fireplace, breakfast, tours

This is one of the best hostels in Ireland, and we'd make a special trip to these otherworldly islands just to stay here.

There. We said it.

This family-run combination of B&B and hostel gets the highest possible marks for friendliness—and for bringing international travelers to a hauntingly beautiful place and taking good care of them. Nice airy dorms, clean bathrooms, super service. Pay a little extra for the B&B option if you're honeymooning, but even in the dorms you'll enjoy yourself.

Gestalt: Bru crew
Hospitality:
Cleanliness:
Party index:

Guests are a combination of Irish weekenders and amazed foreigners, and they usually meet in the terrific restaurant attached to the hostel; it saves you the trouble of cooking, isn't expensive at all, and feeds you plenty of hearty Irish fare. The other gathering place, the common room inside the hostel building, is also wonderfully homey and warmed by (what else?) smoky turf fires that fend off the usual damp chill to the air.

What to do here? Well, this isn't the most touristed of the three islands, so go ahead and act like a local: Take walks around the deserted, rocky place, then hit a few pubs at night for a raucous, friendly time. This hostel's the perfect, low-cost base to do it from. Or take one of the curragh (boat) tours arranged by the hostel.

Just make sure you call ahead in summer, 'cause even though this hostel's pretty new the word's getting out fast!

how to get there:

By ferry: Call hostel for directions.

kilronan hostel

Kilronan, Inishmore Island, Aran Islands, Co. Galway

Phone Number: 099–61255
Rates: €13 per person (about $13 US)
Beds: Contact hostel for current number.
Private/family rooms: None
Season: April 15 to October 31
Affiliation: None
Extras: Fireplace, bike rentals

Popular though simple, this place fills fast on summer weekends. The most striking feature of the place is its second-floor location above a local pub;

Hospitality:
Party index:

beer and music (and the associated noise) are just a couple steps away.

how to get there:

By bus: Call hostel for transit route.
By car: Call hostel for directions.
By train: Call hostel for transit route.

mainistir house hostel

Kilronan, Inishmore Island, Aran Islands, Co. Galway

Phone Number: 099–61169
Fax: 099–61351
Rates: €12–€20 per person (about $12–$20 US); doubles €32 (about $32 US)
Beds: Contact hostel for current number.
Private/family rooms: 6
Affiliation: None
Extras: Breakfast, meals ($), laundry, free pickups, bike rentals

This place is good, with one caveat: We've heard reports about unfriendly staff sometimes. That aside, though, it's a fine hostel with great dinners for sale

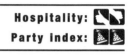

and filling breakfasts included with the rack rate. Plus, it's just half a mile's walk from the Inishmore ferry dock on Galway Bay; the hostel itself overlooks the bay, in fact.

You can buy special Irish Ferries deals that combine your ferry ticket with a night's stay here.

how to get there:

By ferry: From Rosseveal (outside Galway), take ferry (phone: 091–561–767) to Inishmore; walk uphill ½ mile west from dock to hostel.

hynes hostel

Aughrim, Ballinasloe, Co. Galway

Phone Number: 0905–73734
Fax: 0905–73734
Rates: €11.50 per person (about $11.50 US); doubles €30 (about $30 US)
Beds: 12
Private/family rooms: 2
Affiliation: IHH
Extras: Camping, laundry, pickups, bike rentals, piano, fireplace

This is another of those blessed (or cursed, depending on your point of view) hostels attached directly to a pub. There's often traditional

music going on—a godsend, we say, and let's raise a glass to it! If you want quiet, though, you might

try elsewhere—especially since there's an in-house piano that often gets a workout.

Among the other amenities are two private rooms, a campground, a laundry, and bikes for hire.

History buffs will want to check out the Battle of Aughrim Centre, which highlights a tussle that happened back in 1691; it's literally steps from the hostel door.

how to get there:

By bus: Call hostel for transit route.
By car: Call hostel for directions.
By train: Call hostel for transit route.

ben lettery (12 bens) hostel

Ballinafad, Clifden, Co. Galway

Phone Number: 095–51136
Fax: 095–51136
Rates: €10.50–€14.00 per HI member (about $11.00–$14.00 US)
Credit cards: None
Beds: 50
Private/family rooms: Yes
Kitchen available: Yes
Office hours: 7:00 to 10:30 A.M.; 5:00 P.M. to midnight
Season: March 28 to September 30
Affiliation: HI-AO
Extras: Shop

A sturdy white building at the base of one of Connemara's many crags, this place serves up just what you'd expect: clean beds, fifty in all, during summer only.

Remember that this hostel is quite a bit outside Clifden, the unofficial capital of the Connemara, rather than actually in it. So strap on those walking shoes.

Gestalt: Ben there
Party index:

how to get there:

By bus: From Galway, take bus toward Clifden and get off at hostel.
By car: Call hostel for directions.
By train: From Galway Station, 40 miles away, take bus to Clifden.

brookside hostel

Fair Green, Clifden, Co. Galway

Phone Number: 095–21812
Fax: 095–22139
E-mail: brooksidehostel@eircom.net
Rates: €11.50–€15.00 per person (about $11.50–$15.00 US); doubles €30 (about $30 US)
Credit cards: None
Beds: 35
Private/family rooms: Sometimes
Season: March 1 to October 31
Affiliation: IHH
Extras: Laundry, ferry tickets, bike rentals

Hospitality:
Cleanliness:
Party index:

This one's by the river and is pretty basic, offering two private rooms and enough bunkrooms to accommodate about thirty more hostellers besides.

A laundry is clean and well kept.

how to get there:

By bus: Bus stop in Clifden. From stop, walk 2 blocks to hostel.
By car: Call hostel for directions.
By train: Call hostel for transit route.

clifden town hostel

Market Street, Clifden, Co. Galway

Phone Number: 095–21076
Fax: 095–21642
Rates: €11–€12 per person (about $11–$12 US); doubles €30–€34 (about $30–$34 US)
Credit cards: Yes
Beds: 34

Private/family rooms: 3
Affiliation: IHH
Extras: Bike rentals

Gestalt: Our town **Hospitality:**  **Cleanliness:**  **Party index:** 	This place fits the bill in Clifden, offering some standard dorm rooms and three private rooms on top of that. Everything's kept clean and fresh, if simple; you can rent a bike here to explore the area.

Make a special note to book ahead if you're planning a visit late in the summertime, as the town becomes a beehive of activity during a much-anticipated annual pony show.

how to get there:

By bus: Call hostel for transit route.
By car: Call hostel for directions.
By train: Call hostel for transit route.

key to icons

 Attractive natural setting

 Ecologically aware hostel

 Superior kitchen facilities or cafe

 Offbeat or eccentric place

 Superior bathroom facilities

 Romantic private rooms

 Comfortable beds

 A particularly good value

 Wheelchair accessible

Good for business travelers

Especially well suited for families

 Good for active travelers

 Visual arts at hostel or nearby

 Music at hostel or nearby

Great hostel for skiers

 Bar or pub at hostel or nearby

Editors' choice: among our very favorite hostels

doolin

It's hard to believe that such a small town could become so popular in such a short time. But it did and it is—as a result, there are amazingly four hostels in the hamlet. Once you see the local pubs and hear some genuine music, though, you'll certainly understand why.

As you'd expect, hostels here are very good indeed.

doolin hostels
at a glance

HOSTEL	RATING	COST	IN A WORD	PAGE
Aille River Hostel	◩	€11.50–€12.00	cool	146
Rainbow Hostel	◩	€11.00–€12.00	hip	149
Paddy's Doolin Hostel	◩	€12.00	nice	148
Flanagan's Village Hostel		€11.00–€11.50	new	147

aille river hostel ◩

Doolin, Co. Clare

Phone Number: 06570–74260
E-mail: ailleriver@esatclear.ie
Rates: €11.50–€12.00 per person (about $12.00 US); doubles €27–€30 (about $27–$30 US)
Beds: 30
Private/family rooms: Yes
Season: February 20 to January 10

Affiliation: IHH
Extras: Laundry, bike rentals, camping, fireplace, pickups

Gestalt: Doolin banjos
Hospitality:
Party index:

This laid-back farmhouse hostel is Doolin's top bunk, except in fall and early winter, when it reportedly can get a little nippy. A fireplace helps keep the common area warm year-round, though, and the staff is really kind. Heck, the laundry's free! Gotta love that. Besides the regular dorms, three private rooms are a little more comfortable for sleeping, and linen is included.

Doolin itself? As we warned you above, droves of others will be there besides you; don't expect to "discover" it alone. Still, the music and Irish culture here are almost unparalleled. Food, beer, music . . . it all flows. For a getaway—though, again, lots of Americans will have turned up here mysteriously, too—take a hike along the "old road" to the Cliffs of Moher, the abrupt end of Ireland. Not for those who don't like heights.

how to get there:

By bus: Call hostel for transit route.
By car: Near Aille River, between the two villages of Doolin.
By train: Call hostel for transit route.

flanagan's village hostel

Doolin, Co. Clare

Phone Number: 065–707–4654
Rates: €11.50–€12.00 per person (about $11.00–$12.00 US); doubles €28–€30 (about $28–$30 US)
Beds: 24
Private/family rooms: 2
Kitchen available: Yes
Affiliation: IHH
Extras: Laundry

Not exactly right downtown, this hostel is not far either. Word on the street has it that it's another good place, including a kitchen and comfortable common area and sheets in the overnight rate. We'll wait and see whether it develops into another surefire Doolin winner.

Party index:

how to get there:

By bus: Call hostel for transit route.
By car: Call hostel for directions.
By train: Call hostel for transit route.

paddy's doolin hostel

Fisher Street, Doolin, Co. Clare

Phone Number: 065–7074006
E-mail: doolinhostel@eircom.net
Rates: €12 per person (about $12 US); doubles €35 (about $35 US)
Beds: 95
Private/family rooms: 2
Season: January 15 to December 15
Affiliation: IHH
Extras: Bike rentals, laundry, meals ($), pickups, bureau de change, tours

Gestalt: Peppermint Paddy
Hospitality:
Cleanliness:
Party index:

This big, efficiently run hostel is a bit antiseptic. However, you might find such professionalism good if you're here to book a serious outdoors-style holiday. They have a tennis court, rent bikes, and can arrange package tours of the area. It's also the closest hostel to the Cliffs of Moher trail, which the faint of heart can skip.

Otherwise, dorms are the normal deal; there are some private rooms, and they offer laundry and sometimes exchange currency.

how to get there:

By bus: Call hostel for pickup.
By car: Call hostel for directions.
By train: Call hostel for pickup.

rainbow hostel

Toonellin, Doolin, Co. Clare

Phone Number: 065–707–4415
Rates: €11–€12 per person (about $11–$12 US); doubles €26–€28 (about $26–$28 US)
Beds: 16
Private/family rooms: 2
Affiliation: IHH
Extras: Laundry, pickups, fireplace, bike rentals

This might be the hippie hangout in Doolin. We're talking a farmhouse with tents in the yard, turf fires—quintessential Ireland, to be sure. (Although most Irish buildings don't have rooms painted in the colors of the rainbow.) Quarters get kinda tight in the dorms, but the common room is friendly and very laid-back, partly redeeming the place. So do two private rooms.

Gestalt: Rainbow's end
Hospitality:
Party index:

For fun, we'd hit three pubs in a night, sampling different music and beer in each one. You're just about right next to two of the town's finest.

key to icons

 Attractive natural setting

 Ecologically aware hostel

 Superior kitchen facilities or cafe

 Offbeat or eccentric place

 Superior bathroom facilities

 Romantic private rooms

Comfortable beds

 A particularly good value

Wheelchair accessible

Good for business travelers

 Especially well suited for families

 Good for active travelers

 Visual arts at hostel or nearby

Music at hostel or nearby

Great hostel for skiers

Bar or pub at hostel or nearby

Editors' choice: among our very favorite hostels

how to get there:

By bus: Call hostel for pickup.
By car: Call hostel for directions.
By train: Call hostel for pickup.

abbey tourist hostel

Harmony Row, Ennis, Co. Clare

Phone Number: 065–6822260
Fax: 065–6823007
Rates: €14–€20 per person (about $14–$20 US)
Beds: 80
Private/family rooms: Yes
Affiliation: IHO
Extras: Meals ($), laundry, garden

Across the bridge from the well-known Ennis village abbey, this hostel is simple in the IHH style but well run nevertheless. Meals are served, and there's a laundry, too, as well as four private rooms.

Insiders' tip: Walking in Dromore Wood
Gestalt: Abbey road
Cleanliness:
Party index:

Ennis town is your best bet to stock up on grub and tourist info before shoving off into rural and remote Clare, as it's the biggest town for miles and miles. Besides the friary, the banks, and the stores, though, there's little to keep you around for long. However, we did note that the town runs ceilidhs (traditional folk dances) each Wednesday and Saturday night. Definitely try to get to one.

how to get there:

By bus: Call hostel for pickup.
By car: Call hostel for directions.
By train: Call hostel for pickup.

galway

Galway's star is rising. Once a working-class place way out on the west coast, today it's increasingly a destination for hostellers skipping from Dublin to the rest of Ireland. It's easy to get here by train or bus.

Largely as a result of this new influx of young travelers, Galway must now have more hostels per capita than any other city in the world: Amsterdam, eat your heart out. Depending on the year, I've seen anywhere from ten to sixteen hostels in summertime. More seem to pop up all the time, while some old favorites have recently closed.

But what's the problem? In a country just crammed full of great hostels, Galway's really hurting. Must be the demand. We've seen it before: In cities where people would pay twenty bucks to sleep in a paper bag (like San Francisco, Paris, and Galway), the quality of hostels slides downhill.

So while there are quite a good number of hostels in town, not many of them reach the high standard set in much of the rest of Ireland. Our advice? Pay careful attention—and know what you're getting into before you get there.

galway hostels
at a glance

HOSTEL	RATING	COST	IN A WORD	PAGE
Sleepzone	◹	€14.00–€50.00	modern	158
Kinlay House Hostel	◹	€10.00–€20.00	thoughtful	156
Galway Summer Hostel	◹	€14.50	decent	155
Barnacles Quay Street Hostel		€11.50–€19.50	good	152
Salmon Weir Hostel		€10.00–€15.00	central	158
Eyre Square Hostel		€13.00–€15.00	snug	154
Arch View Hostel		€10.00	worn	152
Corrib Villa		€15.00	tired	154
Celtic Tourist Hostel		€16.00–€26.00	shabby	153

arch view hostel

1 Upper Dominick Street, Galway, Co. Galway

Phone Number: 091–586–661
Rates: €10 per person (about $10 US)
Beds: 60
Private/family rooms: None
Affiliation: None
Extras: Internet access

This place is a tough call. It's a beautiful building, sure, tucked in a

Hospitality: [icon]
Party index: [icon]

quiet canal-side spot. And you're in great central position, close to tons of Galway's legendary pubs. Management and staff are okay, too.

However, if you're coming for comfort—bringing the family, maybe?—you might wanna jog elsewhere, as the huge dorms and kitchen have all seen much better days. The common room's one possible respite, the nightlife another.

how to get there:

By bus: Call hostel for transit route.

By car: From Eyre Square, take Williamsgate and Shop Streets, past river to Eglinton Canal. Hostel is at junction of Upper and Lower Dominick Streets, west of the Wolfe Tone Bridge.

By train: Call hostel for transit route.

barnacles quay street hostel

10 Quay Street, Galway, Co. Galway

Phone Number: 091–568–644
Fax: 091–568–644
E-mail: qsh@barnacles.ie
Rates: €12–€20 per person (about $12–$20 US); doubles €46–€52 (about $46–$52 US)
Credit cards: Yes
Beds: 109
Private/family rooms: 6

Kitchen available: Yes
Office hours: Twenty-four hours
Affiliation: IHH
Extras: Laundry, fireplace, breakfast

Some of our snoops liked this place, some didn't; you be the judge. Either way, you're very near the young and vibrant pub scene that Galway's getting so famous for, so at least give it an "A" for location.

Insiders' tip:
Hit the Quay's pub

Party index:

The biggest dorm rooms here can tend to get packed but don't feel too stuffy because of their large size. A better bet, though, would be the quad rooms with en-suite bathroom for maximum privacy. Six private double rooms are also a good bet and all prices include linens. The kitchen is better organized than we'd expected it to be.

how to get there:

By bus: From train station, walk through Eyre Square to Quay Street.
By car: Call hostel for directions.
By train: From train station, walk through Eyre Square to Quay Street.

celtic tourist hostel

Queen Street, Victoria Place, Galway, Co. Galway

Phone Number: 091–566–606
Fax: 091–566–606
Rates: €16–€26 per person (about $16–$26 US)
Beds: 32
Private/family rooms: 6
Kitchen available: Yes
Affiliation: IHO
Extras: Bike rentals, TV, VCR

Not so good, we said after looking this one over. Not terrible, but there are better joints in town by far. At least the kitchen's decent.

Party index:

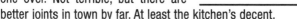

how to get there:

By bus: Call hostel for transit route.
By car: Call hostel for directions.
By train: Call hostel for transit route.

corrib villa hostel

4 Waterside Wood Quay, Galway City, Co. Galway

Phone Number: 091–562–892
Rates: €15 per person (about $15 US)
Beds: 50
Private/family rooms: None
Kitchen available: Yes
Curfew: 3:00 A.M.
Affiliation: None
Extras: Laundry

This is another of Galway's beat-up hostel facilities, balanced by decent management and a lively crowd; take your pick, depending on whether you want comfort or company.

Hospitality:
Party index:

Dorms were too big for our taste, but clean, and the kitchen did impress us despite the crowds.

how to get there:

By bus: Call hostel for transit route.
By car: Call hostel for directions.
By train: Call hostel for transit route.

eyre square hostel

35 Eyre Street, Galway, Co. Galway

Phone Number: 091–568–432
E-mail: manager@eyresquarehostel.com
Rates: €13–€15 per person (about $13–$15 US)
Beds: Contact hostel for current number
Private/family rooms: Yes
Affiliation: None

This new hostel is plunked down right smack in the heart of Galway, featuring your standard wooden bunks and very snug quarters. Some dorms here are as large as twelve and fourteen beds each, but then again others have just two to four beds each—better for families, couples, and small groups.

Gestalt: Eyre head
Party index:

As I've said, it's all about location here. The small building is steps from everything central; you could literally fall out of bed and into some action—not that I'd recommend that.

how to get there:

By bus: From bus terminal, walk to top of Eyre Square and onto Eyre Street. Hostel is opposite Roches Stores, beside Café Revive.

By car: Contact hostel for directions.

By train: From train station, walk to top of Eyre Square and onto Eyre Street. Hostel is opposite Roches Stores, beside Café Revive.

galway summer hostel

St. Mary's College, St. Mary's Road, Galway, Co. Galway

Phone Number: 091–527–411
Fax: 091–528–710
Rates: €14.50 per HI member (about $15 US)
Credit cards: Yes
Beds: 120
Private/family rooms: Yes
Office hours: Twenty-four hours
Season: June 26 to August 24
Affiliation: HI-AO
Extras: Breakfast, meals ($), tours, laundry

Located midway between the two key attractions of Galway Town—the beach and the pubs of Eyre Square—this summer-only An Oige hostel is pretty good.

Cleanliness:
Party index:

Too bad it's only open for two months each year, when St. Mary's College is out of session.

Among the perks: Continental breakfast is included with the price of a bed, and there are some nice family rooms. The place is run as efficiently as most An Oige joints—not a swinging time, maybe, but a clean and safe bed at least.

how to get there:

By bus: From bus station, walk 1 mile along Eyre Square, Shop Street, and across river. Follow Mill Street to New Road; turn left, then left again onto St. Mary's Road, to hostel.

By car: Call hostel for directions.

By train: From Galway Station, walk 1 mile to hostel (directions above).

kinlay house hostel

Merchants Road, Eyre Square, Galway, Co. Galway

Phone Number: 091–565–244
Fax: 091–565–245
E-mail: kinlay.galway@usit.ie
Rates: €10–€20 per person (about $10–$20 US); doubles €45–€49 (about $45–$49 US)
Credit cards: Yes
Beds: 150
Private/family rooms: 15
Office hours: Twenty-four hours
Affiliation: IHH
Extras: Breakfast, meals ($), laundry, bureau de change, on-line booking

Stay here and you'll get great service, but you'll sacrifice a bit in location. Set very close to Galway's train station, the Kinlay House exists

Hospitality:
Cleanliness:
Party Index:

for travelers like us: The no-frills dorms contain up to eight beds, and they're nicely done if plain. Some contain their own bathrooms. For couples, they rent out private rooms at a slight surcharge— kinda like hotel rooms, really.

Everything's clean and laid-back without devolving into Slacker City, and they throw in a bit of continental breakfast for nothin' extra.

Better still, there's an attached budget travel agency right down-stairs—plus tourist information across the street.

how to get there:

By bus: Call hostel for transit route.
By car: Call hostel for directions.
By train: Call hostel for transit route.

Kinlay House Hostel
Galway, Co. Galway
(Photo courtesy of Independent Holiday Hostels of Ireland)

the salmon weir hostel

St. Vincent's Avenue, Woodquay, Galway, Co. Galway

Phone Number: 091–561–133 or 091–522–653
Rates: €10–€15 per person (about $10–$15 US)
Beds: 40
Private/family rooms: 3
Kitchen available: Yes
Curfew: 3:00 A.M.
Affiliation: IHO
Extras: Laundry

Cleanliness: 	
Hospitality:	
Party index:	

This IHO hostel was okay with us, if a bit small.

The kitchen and common area, as usual, are the prime social mixing areas. Good beds and a central location help nudge this one up the list—and the staff really seems to take pains to make it a fun place. And you don't have to fork over extra for sheet rental.

how to get there:

By bus: From bus station, turn left on Eyre Street; walk to Eglinton Street, then turn right on St. Vincent's Avenue.

By car: Call hostel for directions.

By train: From Galway Station, turn left on Eyre Street; walk to Eglinton Street, then turn right on St. Vincent's Avenue.

sleepzone

Bothar Na mBan, Woodquay, Galway, Co. Galway

Phone Number: 091–566–999
Fax Number: 091–566–996
E-mail: info@sleepzone.ie
Rates: €14–€50 per person (about $14–$50 US), doubles €40–€55 (about $40–$55 US)
Beds: 200
Family/private rooms: Yes

Kitchen available: Yes
Affiliation: None
Extras: Internet access ($), parking, TV lounge, courtyard, breakfast, meals
($), tours

This brand-new Galway hostel is getting rave reviews from everyone
for its modernity, friendliness, amenities, and the range of rooming
options. Just off busy Eyre Square,
the hostel is packed with everything   **Party index:**
from pricey single rooms to doubles,
quads, six-bed dorms, and eight- and ten-bed rooms. Most of them
have bathroom facilities en-suite; say bye-bye to gang-style show-
ering, at least for a few nights.

The kitchen is a huge bonus, the lounge features a high-tech TV,
and breakfast is included with your stay. Staff can arrange day tours
to the Aran Islands and similar outings if you wish.

how to get there:

By bus: From city bus terminal, exit station and cross Eyre Square.
Turn right at Cuba Bar; make next left onto Bothar Na mBan, and continue less than 100 yards to hostel on left.

By car: From Dublin, take Dublin Road into Galway, following signs
for Clifden to rotary with traffic lights. Take second exit for city center,
continue ⅓ mile and make second left (opposite Dyke Road); continue
50 yards to hostel on right.

By train: From Galway train station, exit station and cross Eyre
Square. Turn right at Cuba Bar; make next left onto Bothar Na mBan,
and continue less than 100 yards to hostel on left.

inishbofin island hostel ◤

Inishbofin Island, Co. Galway

Phone Number: 095–45855
Fax: 095–45855
Rates: €10 per person (about $10 US); doubles €30 (about $30 US)
Beds: 38
Private/family rooms: 4
Kitchen available: Yes
Season: April 1 to October 1

Affiliation: IHH
Extras: Camping, laundry, tours

This hostel, up a small hill from Inishbofin's harbor and ferry dock, fits its laid-back island perfectly: It's great, too.

Thirty nice bunk beds and four private rooms fill the house, which is as friendly as the locals and travelers who find this speck of rock each summer for good times. There's an amazing pub scene for such a tiny place, and you'll surely meet Irish and Europeans alike.

Gestalt: Island life
Hospitality:
Cleanliness:
Party index:

Don't forget to use the good kitchen and the even better sitting room. Tours can be arranged by the management if you want to know even more about the island.

how to get there:

By ferry: From Cleggan, take ferry to Inishbofin Island; walk ⅓ mile to hostel.

katie o'connor's hostel

Frances Street, Kilrush, Co. Clare

Phone Number: 065–905–1133
Fax: 065–908–0761
E-mail: katieoconnors@eircom.net
Rates: €11–€12 per person (about $11–$12 US); doubles €26–€27 (about $26–$27 US)
Beds: 28
Private/family rooms: 2
Kitchen available: Yes
Season: March 15 to November 1
Affiliation: IHH
Extras: Meals ($), laundry, fireplace

Homey and historic, too, this place fits the bill when in tiny Kilrush. The stars are two good private rooms that can hold up to four, but really any bunk will be okay here.

The common-room fireplace is the usual gathering place for hostellers, and the kitchen's nice, too.

Kilrush itself is considered the capital of west Clare; once a big trading post (lots of steamships used to dock here), it has morphed into a combination market/resort town.

Hospitality: ⬛

Party index: ⬛⬛

how to get there:

By bus: Call hostel for transit route.
By car: Call hostel for directions.
By train: Call hostel for transit route.

doorus house hostel

Doorus, Kinvara, Co. Galway

Phone Number: 091–637512
Fax: 091–637512
Rates: €10.50–€14.00 per HI member (about $11.00–$14.00 US)
Credit cards: None
Beds: 56
Private/family rooms: None
Office hours: 7:00 to 10:00 A.M.; 5:00 to 11:00 P.M.
Affiliation: HI-AO
Extras: Meeting room

Not actually in downtown Kinvara but across a bay from it, this two-story hostel was the former home of Count Florimond de Basterot, whose literary groups—a bunch that included W. B. Yeats—met here, and one group eventually established the renowned Abbey Theatre. Don't know if they'd have enjoyed sleeping eight or ten to a room, but there you have it.

It's standard-issue stuff, quite close to the bleak Burren topography and a nice peninsula with good beaches. Caves and hot springs run through the area as well, so ignore the plainness of

Party index: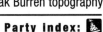

the hostel and strike out for the wild. Hostel staff can help you find out where.

how to get there:

By bus: From Galway, take bus toward Doolin and Ballyvaughan to hostel.

By car: Call hostel for directions.

By train: From Galway Station, 18 miles away, take bus toward Ballyvaughan to Nogra Cross; walk 1 mile to hostel.

lahinch hostel

Church Street, Lahinch, Co. Clare

Phone Number: 065–70648
Fax: 065–7081040
E-mail: lahinchok@eircom.net
Rates: €15–€17 per person (about $15–$17 US); doubles €30–€34 (about $30–$34 US)
Beds: 48
Private/family rooms: 3
Affiliation: IHH
Extras: Laundry, meals ($), breakfast, bike rentals

Next to a church in tiny Lahinch, this place has what you need: clean dorms, a choice of private rooms, bike rentals, a laundry, and meal service. There is sometimes a curfew, however. Check for times.

You only come to Lahinch for one reason: a great—if chilly—beach that's better suited to walking than sunbathing. Locals claim the submarine was invented near here, too, but there isn't exactly a monument sticking up out of the Atlantic to commemorate it.

Just to the north stand the famous Cliffs of Moher, which stretch for 5 miles along the coast and drop as much as 700 feet straight down into the Atlantic. Yikes! You can even climb a viewing tower perched on top of those cliffs—though why the heck would you want to do that? Not for acrophobes, we'd guess.

Insiders' tip:
Aquarium in town

Hospitality:
Cleanliness:
Party index:

how to get there:

By bus: Call hostel for transit route.
By car: Call hostel for directions.
By train: Call hostel for transit route.

old monastery hostel

Letterfrack, Co. Galway

Phone Number: 095–41132
Fax: 095–41680
E-mail: oldmon@indigo.ie
Rates: €12–€13 per person (about $12–$13 US); doubles €30–€32 (about $30–$32 US)
Beds: 50
Private/family rooms: 4
Affiliation: IHH
Extras: Breakfast, meals ($), camping, laundry, bike rentals, pickups

This place is a good place to stay if you're going to be tramping around in the Connemara National Park, especially since they offer awesome veggie

Gestalt: This Old House
Hospitality:
Party index: 🎉🎉

meals, a nice breakfast, a laundry, bikes, sheets included, and a campground—everything the weary hiker needs for a nice stay. Check out the interesting decor, everything from stones to art covering the interior of the place.

There are four private rooms, too. The town is pretty if small, as good a base as we can think of for exploring Connemara.

how to get there:

By bus: Call hostel for transit route.
By car: Call hostel for directions.
By train: Call hostel for transit route.

summerville-westbourne holiday hostel

Dock Road, Limerick, Co. Limerick

Phone Number: 061–302–500
Fax: 061–302–539
E-mail: info@summerwest.com
Rates: €17–€23 per person (about $17–$23 US)

Credit cards: Yes
Beds: 92
Private/family rooms: Yes
Kitchen available: Yes
Affiliation: IHO
Extras: Laundry, bike rentals, breakfast, meals ($), tennis, pool table, TV, fax service, luggage storage

Top kudos to these twin hostels, the poshest in town. These are astonishingly clean and well-run places, with private rooms, excellent

Hospitality:
Party Index:

showers, lots of parking, and a great big kitchen and dining room. Great staff keep things running.

The rooms come in single, double, and dorm configurations, all with en-suite bathrooms and all gorgeous—and no bunk beds! A continental breakfast is included with your price, and they offer professional services like a fax machine and friendly facilities like a pool room. The only complaint we heard, and it was a tiny one: It's a bit of a hike to the city center. Make that more than a bit of a hike.

Riverside Limerick, we should point out, has been experiencing a renaissance in recent years. Besides the local castles and lakes, a rejuvenated arts scene is taking hold here.

how to get there:

By bus: From station walk up Mallow Street, turn left on Dock Road. Hostel is one block from turn on left.
By car: Call hostel for directions.

liscannor village hostel

Liscannor, Co. Clare

Phone Number: 065–708–1550
Fax: 065–708–1417
Rates: €10 per person (about $10 US); doubles €30 (about $30 US)
Beds: 76
Private/family rooms: 4
Season: April 1 to October 30

Affiliation: IHH
Extras: Camping, bike rentals, meals ($)

Nicely situated near a set of real-life Irish pubs, this hostel packs in almost eighty hostellers; go for one of the four private rooms if you can.

Good beer and music are everywhere, and the hostel's central to all. Vaughan's and McHugh's are the undisputed stars of the local pub scene, but you really can't go wrong anywhere in town, we suspect.

The beach at nearby Lahinch is also a popular visit.

how to get there:

By bus: Call hostel for transit route.
By car: Call hostel for directions.
By train: Call hostel for transit route.

oughterard's canrawer house hostel

Station Road, Oughterard, Co. Galway

Phone Number: 091–552–388
Fax: 091–552–388
Rates: €13 per person (about $13 US); doubles €34 (about $34 US)
Beds: 46
Private/family rooms: 1
Kitchen available: Yes
Season: February 1 to October 30
Affiliation: IHH
Extras: Meals ($), laundry, boat rentals, fishing trips, pickups

This place's chief draw is the odd combination of an especially good kitchen and boat rentals for fishing trips with the manager. Dorms range in size from five to about ten beds each. Meals and laundry are offered, and you can also scrap for the one private room if you like.

Hospitality: 👍
Party index: 🎉

What to do around here? There's a pretty neat castle called Aughnanure a couple miles away; walk if you have to, but don't miss it.

how to get there:

By bus: Call hostel for pickup.
By car: Call hostel for directions.
By train: Call hostel for transit route.

galway shannonside schoolhouse hostel 👍

St. Brigid's Road, Portumna, Co. Galway

Phone Number: 050–941–032
Fax: 050–941–060
E-mail: galwayshannonside@eircom.net
Rates: €17 per person (about $17 US); doubles €34–€44 (about $34–$44 US)
Credit cards: None
Beds: 49
Private/family rooms: Yes
Season: February 1 to October 31
Affiliation: IHH
Extras: Breakfast, meals ($), bike rentals

Right by the Shannon River where the river empties into Lough Derg, this schoolhouse looks like a winner to us. Nicely furnished, it includes some rooms with bathrooms attached. They've got singles and doubles in addition to the dorms.

Gestalt: Cool School
Hospitality: 👍
Cleanliness: 👍
Party index: 🎉🎉

They serve meals, include free breakfast, and rent out bikes, too. Don't forget to check out the local castle, the site of an annual Heritage Week celebration in early September.

how to get there:

By bus: Contact hostel for transit route.
By car: Contact hostel for directions.
By train: Contact hostel for transit route.

killary harbour hostel

Rosroe, Renvyle, Co. Galway

Phone Number: 095–43417
Rates: €10.50–€14.00 per HI member (about $10.50–$14.00 US)
Credit cards: None
Beds: 44
Private/family rooms: None
Office hours: 7:00 to 10:00 A.M.; 5:00 P.M. to midnight
Season: March 28 to May 30, weekends only; June 1 to September 30, daily;
Affiliation: HI-AO
Extras: Store

This hostel is very, very plain—a whitewashed fading little building at a tiny harbor in the absolute middle of nowhere.

Though the hostel kinda bites, this is a harbor with a little history to tell.

The German philosopher Wittgenstein wrote his seminal work Philosophical Investigations here in 1948, staring for hours out at one of Ireland's few true fjords. (There wasn't a hostel here then, you understand.)

A visitor's options haven't changed much since those days. Sit mesmerized by the fishing boats tying up, buy food supplies at the small hostel shop, or try out the nice walking trail nearby. Or just gaze, opened-mouthed at the view of Mweelrea, a cliff rising steeply out of the water.

Gestalt:
Private investigations
Cleanliness:
Party Index:

The five dorms contain either eight or ten beds each. An adventure center next door books biking, walking, and other tours of this beautiful but forbidding area.

how to get there:

By bus: From Galway, take bus 50 miles toward Renvyle to Salrock Cross; walk 3 miles to hostel.

By car: Take N59 from Galway or Westport; follow signs to hostel.

By train: From Galway Station, take bus 50 miles toward Renvyle to Salrock Cross; walk 3 miles to hostel.

jamaica inn hostel

Mount Levers, Sixmilebridge, Co. Clare

Phone Number: 061–369220
Fax: 061–369377
E-mail: jamaica@iol.ie
Rates: €12–€17 per person (about $12–$17 US)
Credit cards: Yes
Beds: 40
Private/family rooms: Yes
Office hours: 8:00 A.M. to 8:00 P.M.
Affiliation: IHO, IHH, IH-PO
Extras: Meals ($), bike rentals, laundry

Owners Mike and Nuala constructed this yellow place in the Clare countryside. Just 7 miles from Shannon Airport, it's another one of those hostels that makes a good first night in Ireland if you want to ease into the experience and ease out of your jet lag.

Gestalt: Jamaica plain
Hospitality:
Party index:

They've got everything from single rooms up to ten-bed dorms. Otherwise it has nothing in common with Jamaica, as far as we could tell.

how to get there:

By bus: From Limerick or Shannon Airport, contact hostel for transit details.

By car: Take N18 or N19 to R471.

By train: Contact hostel for transit route.

key to icons

 Attractive natural setting

 Ecologically aware hostel

 Superior kitchen facilities or cafe

 Offbeat or eccentric place

 Superior bathroom facilities

 Romantic private rooms

 Comfortable beds

 A particularly good value

 Wheelchair accessible

 Good for business travelers

 Especially well suited for families

 Good for active travelers

 Visual arts at hostel or nearby

 Music at hostel or nearby

 Great hostel for skiers

 Bar or pub at hostel or nearby

 Editors' choice: among our very favorite hostels

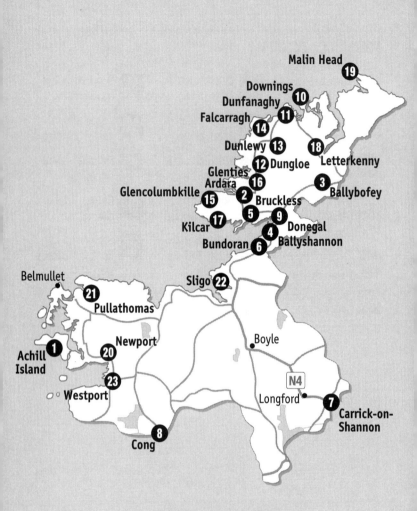

northwestern ireland

Northwestern Ireland—don't you dare confuse this with Northern Ireland, which (as we all know) is officially, if uneasily, part of the United Kingdom—is often overlooked by foreigners. But it's darned popular with the Irish, and with good reason. The place is pretty spectacular, as scenic as anything else in the country, and less touristed because it's so far off the beaten track.

The hostels here are a varied lot; some are superb, but a number of them are just fair at best.

railway hostel

Achill Sound, Achill Island, Co. Mayo

Phone Number: 098–45187
Fax: 098–45550
Rates: €11 per person (about $11 US)
Beds: 16
Private/family rooms: 1
Kitchen available: Yes
Affiliation: IHO
Extras: Laundry, breakfast ($), bike rentals, meals ($), camping

Party index:  This plain hostel's near a pub, which is nice, and all dorms and the private room come with en-suite bathrooms.

Have fun with a friend and try this: Each set up in one of the dueling kitchens, then see who can boil the spaghetti first.

On second thought, don't bother.

how to get there:

By bus: Call hostel for transit route.
By car: Call hostel for directions.

valley house hostel & bar

Dugort, Achill Island, Co. Mayo

Phone Number: 098–47204
Fax: 098–47334
E-mail: info@valley-house.com
Rates: €11–€15 per person (about $11–$15 US)
Beds: 25
Private/family rooms: 2
Season: March 15 to October 31
Affiliation: IHO
Extras: Fireplace, pub, camping, laundry, showers ($), golf

Located near sandy beaches on the northern end of Achill Island, this hostel features an in-house bar and your usual, very standard, quad rooms.

Party index: 🎉🎉🎉

The house has quite an interesting history, though: Its owner was murdered and a novel was later based on her life.

how to get there:

By bus: Call hostel for transit route.
By car: Call hostel for directions.

wayfarer hostel

Keel, Achill Island, Co. Mayo

Phone Number: 098–43266
Fax: 098–43266
E-mail: wayfarerhostel@iolfree.ie
Rates: €10.50 per person (about $11.00 US); doubles €24 (about $24 US)
Beds: 32
Private/family rooms: 4
Season: March 14 to October 6
Affiliation: IHH, IHO
Extras: Laundry

Open only part of the year, this island joint has the advantage of being near one of Ireland's better beaches—and it's got enough fans that you're sure to meet someone interesting. There are also four private rooms and a laundry.

Gestalt: Way to go
Hospitality: 🛏️
Party index: 🎉🎉🎉

The resorty island, the country's biggest, has some incredible cliff-side scenery that you could bike or drive in good weather.

how to get there:

By bus: Call hostel for transit route.
By car: Call hostel for directions.

wild haven hostel 🛏️

The Points, Achill Sound, Achill Island, Co. Mayo

Phone Number: 098–45392
Rates: €13 per person (about $13 US); doubles €34–€38 (about $34–$38 US)
Beds: Contact hostel for current number.
Private/family rooms: 4
Lockout: 11:30 A.M. to 3:30 P.M.
Affiliation: None
Extras: Meals ($), fireplace, campground, laundry

This is the nicest hostel of the quartet on Achill Island—a beautifully furnished house outfitted with little touches like quilts, a cozy fireplace, and such. They serve delicious dinners, too, that would keep us coming back for more. A campground is also available for pinchpenny hostellers.

Gestalt: Wild at heart
Hospitality:
Party index:

how to get there:

By bus: Call hostel for transit route.
By car: Call hostel for directions.

drumbarron hostel

The Diamond, Ardara, Co. Donegal

Phone Number: 074–9541200
Rates: €11–€12 per person (about $11–$12 US)
Beds: 16
Private/family rooms: 1
Affiliation: IHO
Extras: Laundry, bike rentals
Curfew: 1:00 A.M.

Smack in a popular weaving area of Donegal, this is an adequate but boring place to put your head right in the center of Ardara. You check in across the way, not at the hostel, and there is practically nothing "extra" about this place.

Gestalt: Sheepish
Party index:

A good museum nearby explains the history and method of weaving and dying wool in more detail than you thought possible.

how to get there:

By bus: Call hostel for transit route.
By car: Call hostel for directions.

finn farm hostel

Cappry, Ballybofey, Co. Donegal

Phone Number: 074–9132261
Fax: 074–9132261
Rates: €11–€12 per person (about $11–$12 US)
Beds: 20
Private/family rooms: 10
Affiliation: IHO
Extras: Bike rental, camping, laundry, meals ($)

Located a mile outside Ballybofey, this hostel is surprisingly well stocked with bikes, laundry, meal service, and a campground. It's a good rustic choice.

Gestalt: Finny fun
Party index: 🎉

how to get there:

By bus: Call hostel for transit route.
By car: Call hostel for directions.
By train: Call hostel for transit route.

duffy's hostel

Donegal Road, Ballyshannon, Co. Donegal

Phone Number: 072–51535
Rates: €10 per person (about $10 US); doubles €26 (about $26 US)
Beds: 12
Private/family rooms: 1
Season: March 1 to October 15
Affiliation: IHH
Extras: Camping, bike rental, bookstore

Interestingly, there's a used bookstore in the garage at this inexpensive hostel—or at least there used to be. It's a strange place, and that's not all good in this case; we love the management, but we had problems with the worn, sometimes unclean hostel.

Hospitality:
Cleanliness:
Party index:

There's one private room, a few bunks, a camping area, and bikes for hire. Odd and slightly endearing, sure, but definitely missable.

how to get there:

By bus: Call hostel for transit route.
By car: Call hostel for directions.
By train: Call hostel for transit route.

gallagher's farm hostel

Darney, Bruckless, Co. Donegal

Phone Number: 073–9737057
Rates: €12.50 per person (about $13.00 US)
Beds: 18
Private/family rooms: None
Affiliation: IHH
Extras: Laundry, bike rentals

Hospitality:
Party index:

Located in a farm's outbuilding, this place provides a nice taste of rural Ireland. It's simple all right—they don't serve meals anymore—but they have a laundry and bikes for rent.

how to get there:

By bus: Call hostel for transit route.
By car: Call hostel for directions.
By train: Call hostel for transit route.

homefield hostel

Bayview Avenue, Bundoran, Co. Donegal

Phone Number: 072–41288
Fax: 072–41049
E-mail: homefield@indigo.ie
Rates: €16 per person (about $16 US); doubles €32 (about $32 US)
Beds: 30
Private/family rooms: Yes
Affiliation: IHH
Extras: Breakfast, meals ($), TV, tours, outings, horseback trips, bike rentals, pickups

This place once hosted lots of school groups on outings and activities. It appears to have scaled back somewhat on those bookings, and their loss is your

Hospitality:
Party index:

gain. They still serve a free breakfast with your bed and maintain four private rooms. Other meals can be purchased at the hostel restaurant, and they're downright delish.

The owners take pride in the wide range of outdoor activities available through the hostel, which include horseback rides, hikes, fishing trips, and more!

The surrounding area's part tourist schlock, part authentic British Isles, with gift shops alongside real thatched cottages.

how to get there:

By bus: Call hostel for pickup.
By car: Call hostel for directions.
By train: Call hostel for pickup.

town clock hostel

Main Street, Carrick-on-Shannon, Co. Leitrim

Phone Number: 078–21848
Fax: 078–22151
Rates: €15–€18 per person (about $15–$18 US)
Beds: 20

Private/family rooms: Yes
Season: June 1 to September 30
Affiliation: IHO
Extras: Bike rentals, patio
Lockout: 11:30 A.M. to 1:30 P.M.

How to find this place? Simple: Look for the town clock, then look beneath the arch. Easy.

This is a good, if simple, place in the center of Carrick-on-Shannon that rents bikes and maintains a double room of twin beds and a quad room of four bunks in addition to its pair of dormitories. It's justly proud of its courtyard.

Gestalt: Clock of ages
Hospitality:
Party index:

Carrick isn't a bad place to stock up, as there are a couple shops here. Riverboat trips along the Shannon can be booked right in town.

how to get there:

By bus: Call hostel for transit route.
By car: Call hostel for directions.
By train: Call hostel for transit route.

cong hostel

Lisloughrey, Quay Road, Cong, Co. Mayo

Phone Number: 092–46089
Fax: 092–46448
E-mail: quiet.man.cong@iol.ie
Web site: www.quietman-cong.com
Rates: €13 per person (about $13 US); doubles €32 (about $32 US)
Credit cards: Yes
Beds: 56
Private/family rooms: 6
Kitchen available: Yes
Office hours: 7:00 A.M. to midnight
Affiliation: IHH, IHO
Extras: Meals ($), laundry, meeting room, bike rental, camping, TV, movies, shuttle, boat rentals, free pickups

Built as a hostel a mile outside ruggedly located Cong, this joint is pretty well outfitted with a TV, laundry, bike rentals, and campground. Interestingly, they play the John Wayne film The Quiet Man at night; it was filmed here, and is still—many years later—a source of local pride. Long live the Duke.

Gestalt: King Cong
Hospitality:
Cleanliness:
Party index:

Anyhow, dorms are clean and good, some rooms have en-suite bathrooms, the kitchen and common room are things of beauty, and the staff is surprisingly laid-back for a formerly An Oige–affiliated joint. For fun, hit the local lakes (loughs in the local tongue) of Corrib, Cara, and Mask, or take the shuttle into the tiny town. Kids love the on-site playground. Actually, so do the adults.

how to get there:

By bus: From Cork or Galway, take Bus Éireann to Cong; walk 1 mile to hostel.

By car: Call hostel for directions.

By train: Galway Station, 25 miles away, is the closest stop; from Galway, take Bus Éireann to Cong, then walk 1 mile to hostel.

the quiet man hostel

Abbey Street, Cong, Co. Mayo

Phone Number: 092–46089
Fax: 092–46448
E-mail: quiet.man.cong@iol.ie
Rates: €11–€13 per HI member (about $11–$13 US)
Credit cards: Yes
Beds: 104
Private/family rooms: 4
Affiliation: HI-AO
Extras: Laundry, bureau de change, bike rentals, meals ($)

Centrally located and near Cong's lone historical site—a twelfth-century abbey—this handsome house fills fast during its open season.

No wonder: It offers a decent alternative when the other hostel in town (now owned by the same family) is full and offers a laundry and other services. In fact, stay here and you also get access to the other hostel's bigger grounds.

Gestalt:	Quiet riot
Hospitality:	
Party index:	

Also of interest when you're in town are the numerous rivers that lace and practically submerge the town at times; they spring from deep in the earth.

how to get there:

By bus: From Cork or Galway, take Bus Éireann to Cong.
By car: Call hostel for directions.
By train: Galway Station, 25 miles away, is the closest stop; from Galway, take Bus Éireann to Cong, then walk 1 mile to hostel.

donegal

We love Donegal. We admit it. This quiet—yet percolating—town has got what you came for, the legendary Irish "craic" (crack, or atmosphere). In other words, there are plenty of pubs and Irish folk musicians and old codgers hanging out with big glasses of Guinness.

Both hostels here are good and serviceable, providing good bases for further exploration of the area.

donegal hostels
at a glance

HOSTEL	RATING	COST	IN A WORD	PAGE
Donegal Town Hostel		€11.50	happy	182
Ball Hill Hostel		€10.50–€13.50	sylvan	181

ball hill hostel

Donegal Town, Co. Donegal

Phone Number: 073–21174
Fax: 073–22604
Rates: €10.50–€13.50 per HI member (about $11.00–$14.00 US)
Credit cards: None
Beds: 66
Private/family rooms: Yes
Office hours: 7:00 A.M. to midnight
Season: March 28 to September 30, daily; rest of year, weekends only
Affiliation: HI-AO
Extras: Tours, boat trips, outings

A former coast guard station on the north side of Donegal Bay, this An Oige hostel is as squared and white as a block of soap. A two-story block of soap, that is, with eleven plain six-bed dorms.

But it has an absolutely amazing setting. You might not mind the 3-mile walk from town or the bus ride, as well as the isolation, to be near beaches and such incredible views. Give lots of credit to the An Oige staffers here, who defy usual An Oige custom and actually help you out; a variety of tours, trips, and outings are possible. They will even advise hostellers where to get the best mussels at the beach and will prepare a feast afterwards. Walkers like to hit the Blue Stack Mountains or look down from the high cliff called Slieve League nearby.

Insiders' tip:
Good local sweaters

Gestalt: Ball room

Hospitality:

Cleanliness:

Party index:

As befits the soap imagery, it's pretty darned clean, too. Whether it will float in the water, well, we didn't find out.

how to get there:

By bus: Buses run regularly to Donegal from throughout Ireland. From station, walk 3 miles to hostel or change to bus for Killybegs; get off at Ball Hill, and walk 1 mile to hostel.

By car: From Donegal center, drive Killybegs Road for 3 miles, turn left at Texaco, and continue to hostel.

donegal town
independent hostel

Killybegs Road, Doonan, Donegal, Co. Donegal

Phone Number: 074–9722805
Rates: €11.50 per person (about $12.00 US); doubles €27 (about $27 US)
Beds: 40
Private/family rooms: 2
Affiliation: IHH
Extras: Laundry, camping, pickups

A white house located outside central Donegal, this makes a nice laid-back crash pad (or campground) with better-than-usual service; the two private rooms are really in demand, so act fast if you want those. In fact, call ahead for any rooms—the cool management

makes this often the first place in town to fill with happy hostellers. A laundry is also available.

Donegal itself is well known for quality shopping, of all things, in case you're the sort of hosteller who needs to truck home suitcases of stuff from lands you've traveled in.

Need food? Continue on to Killybegs and buy some fresh fish right off the boat at the docks.

how to get there:

By bus: Call hostel for pickup.
By car: Call hostel for directions.
By train: Call hostel for pickup.

tra na rosann hostel

Downings, Co. Donegal

Phone Number: 074–55374 (Booking: 01–830–4555)
Rates: €11.50–€14.00 per HI member (about $12.00–$14.00 US)
Credit cards: None
Beds: 34
Private/family rooms: None

Office hours: 7:00 to 10:00 A.M.; 5:00 P.M. to midnight
Season: June 1 to September 30
Affiliation: HI-AO

This far-northern, chalet-like place scores with good accommodating staff, a beach, and knockout views. Originally a hunting lodge, it opened way back in 1936. It sits atop a hill and squarely in a Gaeltacht (authentically Irish) area. It's worn, sure, but ignore that if you can.

Later, hike or bike around the Rosguill Peninsula, paw through the remains of Doe Castle, or check the Graveyard of the Donegal Chieftains. A good hill walk with views begins at the hostel, too. For food, go to the docks and buy fish from local fishermen.

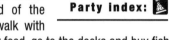
Hospitality:
Party index:

how to get there:

By bus: From Derry, take bus to Letterkenny. Then take Gallaghers Bus (074–37037) to hostel (one daily).
By car: Call hostel for directions.
By train: Derry Station, 45 miles away, is the nearest stop.

key to icons

 Attractive natural setting

 Ecologically aware hostel

 Superior kitchen facilities or cafe

 Offbeat or eccentric place

 Superior bathroom facilities

 Romantic private rooms

 Comfortable beds

 A particularly good value

 Wheelchair accessible

 Good for business travelers

 Especially well suited for families

 Good for active travelers

 Visual arts at hostel or nearby

 Music at hostel or nearby

 Great hostel for skiers

 Bar or pub at hostel or nearby

 Editors' choice: among our very favorite hostels

corcreggan mill hostel

Dunfanaghy, Co. Donegal

Phone Number: 074–36409
Fax: 074–36902
E-mail: millhostel@corcreggan.com
Rates: €11 per person (about $11 US); doubles €28–€30 (about $28–$30 US)
Beds: 28
Private/family rooms: 4
Affiliation: IHH
Extras: Camping, laundry, meals

Pretty nice place here, on the way to Falcarragh. It's rather unusual:

Gestalt: Green acres
Hospitality:
Party index: 🎉🎉

Part is housed inside a mockup of an old railroad station (stone walls here) and the rest in the so-called Kiln House. Coooool.

There's no smoking allowed, and even if it's pretty basic there is an organic garden on the premises. They'll even give you a free vegetarian meal if you help with the chores. Two private rooms add intimacy if you can snag 'em.

Dunfanaghy, as a stop, has a few more fun things than you'd expect: a natural wonder called McSwyne's Gun, good castle ruins, and entertainments like golf and restaurants. Plus the usual pubs.

how to get there:

By bus: Call hostel for transit route.
By car: From Dunfanaghy, take N56 about 2 miles west to New Lake.
By train: Call hostel for transit route.

crohy head hostel

Dungloe, Co. Donegal

Phone Number: 075–21950
Rates: €11–€13 per HI member (about $11–$13 US)
Credit cards: None
Beds: 36

Private/family rooms: Sometimes
Office hours: 7:00 to 10:00 A.M.; 5:00 P.M. to midnight
Season: June 1 to September 30
Affiliation: HI-AO

This simple three-story in a former coast guard station is placed atop a dramatic cliff in an already dramatic walking area, the Crohy Head region. The views here overlook Boylagh Bay and the Atlantic; the area's filled with cliffs and caves. Beaches in the area are also nice.

Gestalt: Head room
Party index: 🎉

The hostel is just blah, though you won't be spending any time there; there are three quad rooms and three bigger ones.

how to get there:

By bus: From Dublin or Derry, take Lough Swilly bus to Dungloe and walk 5 miles along coast to hostel.

By car: Call hostel for directions.

By train: Derry Station, 55 miles away, is the nearest stop.

greene's holiday hostel

Carnmore Road, Dungloe, Co. Donegal

Phone Number: 075–21943
Fax: 075–21943
Rates: €11 per person (about $11 US); doubles €28 (about $28 US)
Beds: 20
Private/family rooms: 6
Affiliation: IHH
Extras: Bike rentals, laundry, campground
Curfew: Yes

Dorms here have six to eight beds each, and there are some additional private rooms to pick from as well. Laundry and bike rentals are also offered at the place, which is really just a base to explore the Crohy Head region.

Gestalt: Green's acres
Party index: 🎉🎉

Book way-y-y-y ahead for July, as a long festival swells the town to unimaginable numbers then.

how to get there:

By bus: Call hostel for transit route.
By car: Call hostel for directions.
By train: Call hostel for transit route.

errigal hostel

Dunlewy, Gweedore, Co. Donegal

Phone Number: 075–31180
Rates: €10.50–€14.00 per HI member (about $11.00–$14.00 US)
Credit cards: None
Beds: 46
Private/family rooms: Yes
Office hours: 7:00 to 10:00 A.M.; 5:00 P.M. to midnight
Affiliation: HI-AO

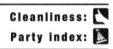

This white house, beside a lake and lying at the foot of Errigal Mountain, makes a decent and spotless launch pad for poking around

Cleanliness: 🗻
Party index: 🎉

County Donegal or walking along the Ulster Way. Glenveagh Castle is right next door, as is a good folk museum and some great sunsets over the so-called Bloody Foreland.

This place is not too bad, with a pleasant country house feel to it. There are four quad rooms, and four bigger ones, from which to pick. Remember that you're more than 2 miles from even a small village, though, so stock up with chow first.

If you're a fan of Celtic music, try to stop at Leo's Tavern in Gweedore. There's authentic Irish music here, sometimes played by owner Leo—whose sons and daughters formed the popular Irish band Clannad. Cool. Gweedore, by the way, is one of the most traditional Gaelic villages in Ireland, possibly; you'll still see and here the language everywhere.

how to get there:

By bus: From Derry or Letterkenny, take Lough Swilly bus toward Dungloe to Dunlewy Cross; walk 2 miles to hostel.
By car: Call hostel for directions.
By train: From Derry, take Lough Swilly bus toward Dungloe to Dunlewy Cross; walk 2 miles to hostel.

shamrock lodge hostel

Main Street, Falcarragh, Co. Donegal

Phone Number: 074–35859
Fax: 074–35192
Rates: €13 per person (about $13 US); doubles €30 (about $30 US)
Beds: 14
Private/family rooms: 2
Season: January 15 to December 15
Affiliation: IHH

Located right above a pub, this small and unquiet place is perfect only for those who came to Ireland to drink in a local pub. Raise your hands. Wow! Okay, in that case it's perfect for almost all of us. The rest of you, well, bring earplugs.

Hospitality:
Party Index:

Seriously, though, the music and beer are just amazing here. On second thought, forget the earplugs: You'll probably spend all night in that fun pub anyway. The hostel's merely adequate, but who cares?

how to get there:

By bus: Call hostel for transit route.
By car: Call hostel for directions.
By train: Call hostel for transit route.

dooey hostel

Glencolumbkille, Co. Donegal

Phone Number: 073–30130
E-mail: dooeyhostel@hostellingireland.com
Rates: €10 (about $10 US); doubles €21 (about $21 US)
Beds: 32
Private/family rooms: 6
Kitchen available: Yes
Affiliation: IHO
Extras: Camping

You can't get much closer to nature than this: Rocks and moss actually line one wall of this hostel, which occupies a spectacular location overlooking the ocean. Planted in a hill with views of the coastline, you'll need to pry your jaw off the floor when you see it. The campsite's even better, if that's possible.

Whatever the dorms and kitchen lack, the location makes up for. Locally, the gaily colored buildings and pubs—filled with real Irish characters, not for-the-benefit-of-tourist types—are superb. If you're passing through in June, try to come June 9, when townspeople make an annual pilgrimage past the many crosses and other religious relics that dot the surrounding countryside.

Insiders' tip:
Fiddle fest in summer

Gestalt: Sea-saw

Party index:

Also don't miss the local folk museum, which is even better than they usually are in Ireland.

how to get there:

By bus: Call hostel for transit route.
By car: Call hostel for directions.
By train: Call hostel for transit route.

campbell's holiday hostel

Glenties, Co. Donegal

Phone Number: 075–51491
Fax: 075–51492
E-mail: campbellshostel@eircom.net
Rates: €12 per person (about $12 US); doubles €28 (about $28 US)
Beds: 42
Private/family rooms: 7
Season: April 1 to October 30
Affiliation: IHH
Extras: Fireplace, laundry, TV, bike rentals

Insiders' tip:
Harvest time is hoppin'

Gestalt: Campbell's soup

Hospitality:

Cleanliness:

Party index:

Right beside Glenties's little museum, this hostel is nicely snug with a fireplace, good kitchen and common room, and seven private rooms—some of which have their own en-suite bathrooms. It's all clean and well done enough.

A small and slightly interesting museum is just steps away.

how to get there:

By bus: Call hostel for transit route.
By car: Call hostel for directions.
By train: Call hostel for transit route.

derrylahan house hostel

Carrick Road, Derrylahan, Kilcar, Co. Donegal

Phone Number: 074–9738079
Fax: 074–9738447
E-mail: derrylahan@eircom.net
Rates: €10 per person (about $10 US); doubles €28 (about $28 US)
Beds: 35
Private/family rooms: 2
Kitchen available: Yes
Affiliation: IHH
Extras: Camping, laundry, pickups, bike rental, store

This place is wildly popular, and just superb—but take heed: It's quite small, so good luck in summer. Plan and book way ahead or cry in your milk for months afterward that you missed out on it.

For starters, it's got a nice location in the countryside: You arrive and realize you're looking out on a sparkling bay. Dorms and private rooms are cheery and comforting; in the morning pick up free tea and

Gestalt: Derry good
Hospitality:
Cleanliness:
Party index:

scones for breakfast. You can buy more food in the good hostel provisions shop—and fix it in a superior kitchen.

For fun during the daytime, you could do any number of hikes. The folks who run this place run a pony riding center, so you could try that, too.

Finally, they really do care about the environment here and do their part to use as few resources as possible. Very well done—one of the best in Ireland.

how to get there:

By bus: Take bus to Carrick or Kilcar, then call hostel for pickup.
By car: From Kilcar, drive 2 miles north on road to Carrick.

port hostel

Orchard Crest, Letterkenny, Co. Donegal

Phone Number: 074–19125315
Fax Number: 074–19125409
E-mail: porthostel@eircom.net
Rates: €12–€18 (about $12 to $18 US)
Beds: 18
Affiliation: IHO
Extras: laundry, tours

This is one of the most sociable hostels in Donegal, thanks to a laid-back groove and a super slate of activities (depending on hostelier interest). The dorms and private rooms are nice enough, and there's even a laundry to wash your dirty stuff.

Gestalt: Port authority
Party index: 🎉🎉🎉

Letterkenny is bigger than it sounds, and more hip, too, thanks to a local university. You won't lack for things to do; hit one of the many pubs, coffee shops, health food stores, or pizzerias for fun, and don't miss the local cathedral, a wonder in and of itself.

how to get there:

By bus: From Derry, take Bus Éireann or Lough Swilly bus service to Letterkenny; from Dublin, take Bus Éireann to Letterkenny.
By car: Contact hostel for directions.
By train: Contact hostel for transit route.

malin head hostel

Malin Head, Inishowen, Co Donegal.

Phone Number: 074–9370309
Rates: €12.50 per person (about $13.00 US), doubles €31 (about $31 US)
Beds: 20
Private/family rooms: Yes
Affiliation: IHH
Extras: Fireplace, organic gardens, reflexology treatments

Out on gorgeous Malin Head, this crunchola-style hostel features an organic garden, fireplace—and the availability of aromatherapy treatments! There's a charge for those, of course. The tiny village of Inishowen, set along the Inishowen 100 scenic route, has

Party Index: 🎉

the requisite post office and pub. But you're probably here to catch sunsets over the rocks and sparkly beaches of the Head or buy fish off the docks. Still bored? Try a taste of the local seaweed, cooked into desserts or just chewed as a salty snack.

Oh, yes, they recycle.

how to get there:

By bus: From Derry or Letterkenny, take Lough Swilly bus service to Malin Head; from Parnell Square in Dublin, take McGinley bus line to to Carndonagh.

By car: Take Inishowen 100 route, following signs to Bridgend and Buncrana; hostel is signed, 6 miles outside Malin Village.

By train: Take train to Derry, then Lough Swilly bus service to Malin Head.

sandrock holiday hostel

Port Ronan Pier, Malin Head, Inishowen, Co. Donegal

Phone Number: 074–9370289
E-mail: sandrockhostel@eircom.net
Rates: €10 per person (about $10 US)
Beds: 20
Private/family rooms: None

Affiliation: IHO, IHH
Extras: Laundry, bike rentals, pickups

Knockout vistas are the chief draw of this small, new-home hostel, which is equipped with the usual dorm beds and a laundry and overlooks miles of ocean and cliff. The staff is good enough to pick you up if you need it, and they offer bikes for rent as well.

Gestalt: North star
Hospitality: 🕯
Cleanliness: 🕯
Party index: 🎉

Malin Head is the Irish Republic's most northerly point and, like we said, you couldn't find better views if you tried.

how to get there:

By bus: Call hostel for transit route.
By car: Call hostel for directions.

traenlaur lodge

Lough Feeagh, Newport, Co. Mayo

Phone Number: 098–41358
Rates: €10–€13 per HI member (about $10–$13 US)
Credit cards: None
Beds: 32
Private rooms: None
Office hours: 7:00 to 10:00 A.M.; 5:00 to 11:00 P.M.
Season: March 28 to May 30, weekends; June 1 to September 30, daily
Affiliation: HI-AO
Extras: Meals ($), shop

A little two-story fishing lodge on a private harbor, this can be fun if you want to feel like an Irishman for a day. Lough Feeagh (i.e., the lake in question) is beautiful, and indoors the hostel maintains a classy feel with touches like flagstone floors.

Gestalt: Go fish
Party index: 🎉

You're actually 5 miles outside Newport, though, so plan to stock up ahead of time; they do cook dinners here for a charge. Fortuitously, the hostel's also situated at the crossroads of two walking trails.

how to get there:

By bus: From Westport, take bus toward Achill to Newport and walk 5 miles to hostel.

By car: Call hostel for directions.

By train: From Westport Station, 35 miles away, take bus toward Achill to Newport and walk 5 miles to hostel.

kilcommon lodge hostel

Pullathomas, Co. Mayo

Phone Number: 097–84621
Fax: 097–84621
E-mail: kilcommonlodge@eircom.net
Rates: €9.50 per person (about $10.00 US); doubles €24 (about $24 US)
Beds: 20
Private/family rooms: 4
Affiliation: IHH
Extras: Meals ($), laundry
Curfew: Midnight
Lockout: 9:00 A.M. to 5:00 P.M.

key to icons

 Attractive natural setting

 Ecologically aware hostel

 Superior kitchen facilities or cafe

 Offbeat or eccentric place

 Superior bathroom facilities

 Romantic private rooms

 Comfortable beds

 A particularly good value

 Wheelchair accessible

Good for business travelers

Especially well suited for families

 Good for active travelers

 Visual arts at hostel or nearby

 Music at hostel or nearby

Great hostel for skiers

 Bar or pub at hostel or nearby

Editors' choice: among our very favorite hostels

This smallish hostel on the Mullet Peninsula includes four double rooms among its twenty standard beds and adds laundry and meal service to the mix. Take note of the daytime lockout. The main thing to do around here is pay someone to take you out in a boat to see the rest of the peninsula.

Insiders' tip:
Anchor Bar
Party index: 🎉

how to get there:

By bus: Call hostel for transit route.
By car: Call hostel for directions.
By train: Call hostel for transit route.

sligo

Sligo's surprisingly large for this part of Ireland, and makes a convenient stock-up stop—and it's on the main train and bus lines.

Above all, this is known as the capital of Yeats country. The Yeats Visitor Centre and the good attached library and art gallery are among the best things to visit here, giving insight not only into the life of a Nobel Prize–winning poet but other Irish writers as well. Yeats's name is almost everywhere you turn, and it can get tiring, but there are some interesting things going on around town, too.

The hostels here vary in quality, as might be expected. But two of the three are darned good, and the other will certainly do.

sligo hostels
at a glance

HOSTEL	RATING	COST	IN A WORD	PAGE
White House Hostel	◣	€10.00	friendly	196
Harbour House	◣	€16.00–€20.00	great	195
Eden Hill Hostel		€11.00–€12.50	adequate	195

eden hill hostel

Pearse Road, Marymount, Sligo Town, Co. Sligo

Phone Number: 071–9143204
E-mail: edenhillhostel@eircom.net
Rates: €11.00–€12.50 per person (about $11.00–$13.00 US); doubles €32–€35 (about $32–$35 US)
Beds: 35
Private/family rooms: 2
Office hours: 8:00 A.M. to midnight
Affiliation: IHH
Extras: Laundry, bike rentals, pickups, camping, TV, VCR

Pretty well outfitted with services, the Victorian-home hostel on top of Eden Hill keeps itself clean. So what if it's a little boring and a little distant from downtown?

Hospitality:
Cleanliness:
Party index:

It's got a laundry, campground, and nice television room, and they will rent you a bike. The thirty-five beds filling five dorms and two private rooms are just fine. However, as we say, it's a little distant—a mile or more—from the transit stations and center of the action. Not the best bed in town, but we'd stay here. It's just fine.

how to get there:

By bus: From bus station, call hostel for pickup or walk to tourist office on Temple Street. Turn up Mail Coach Road and walk about ½ mile, then bear onto Pearse Road; hostel is on right.

By car: Call hostel for directions.

By train: From Sligo Station, call hostel for pickup or walk to tourist office on Temple Street. Turn up Mail Coach Road and walk about ½ mile, then bear onto Pearse Road; hostel is on right.

harbour house hostel

Finisklin Road, Sligo Town, Co. Sligo

Phone Number: 071–9171547
Fax: 071–9171547

E-mail: harbourhouse@eircom.net
Rates: €16–€20 per person (about $16–$20 US); doubles €36–€50 (about $36–$50 US)
Credit cards: Yes
Beds: 48
Private/family rooms: 5
Kitchen available: Yes
Affiliation: IHO, IHH
Extras: Bike rentals, meals ($), laundry

Gestalt: House beautiful
Hospitality:
Party index:

This joint is fast becoming one of the best bets in town, and as long as it doesn't get super overused, it'll remain that way awhile.

Location isn't absolutely central, but it's good enough for us; beds are comfy, rooms are well lit, and kitchen and common space are all usefully thought out.

how to get there:

By bus: Call hostel for transit route.
By car: Call hostel for directions.
By train: Call hostel for transit route.

---

white house hostel

Markievicz Road, Sligo Town, Co. Sligo

Phone Number: 071–9145160
Fax: 071–9144456
Rates: €10 per person (about $10 US)
Beds: 31
Private/family rooms: 1
Affiliation: IHH
Extras: Breakfast, sheets ($)

If you like young backpackers, you'll love this place; there's a nice groovy vibe. If you want families and schoolkids, move along—but we doubt you did.

Actually, this place is pretty good—and, guess what, it comes with a nice bonus river view along with its central Sligo location. A small

Party index:  breakfast is always included with your bed, it feels like home, and folks love to hang in the good common room. One private room is a potential bonus.

For fun? Well, as previously mentioned, this is the heart of Yeats country. And if you're not interested in that, then Sligo's downtown abbey, open from mid-June until mid-September, looks suitably old (as it oughta—it was constructed in the middle 1200s).

how to get there:

By bus: From bus station, take Lord Edward Street across river, then turn left onto Markievicz Road.

By car: Call hostel for directions.

By train: From Sligo Station, take Lord Edward Street across river, then turn left onto Markievicz Road.

club atlantic hostel

Altamount Street, Westport, Co. Mayo

Phone Number: 098–26644 or 098–26717
Fax: 098–26241
Rates: €11.00–€13.50 per person (about $11.00–$14.00 US)
Credit cards: Yes
Beds: 140
Private/family rooms: 15
Office hours: 7:00 A.M. to 2:00 P.M.
Season: March 10 to October 31
Affiliation: HI-AO, IHH
Extras: Meals ($), laundry, camping, store, pool table, video games

A purpose-built hostel right next to the transit station, this recently expanded facility is a convenient spot to rest up for trips to Crogh Patrick, Achill Island, or other spots. In

Party index:  addition to the oodles of good dorms— this is a big place—there are fifteen even better private rooms, even coming with their own en-suite bathrooms as a bonus. You also get access to the hotel pool nearby, though it costs a bit extra. (You didn't really come to Ireland to swim, did you?)

This cute little town has an octagonal main square and several other nice areas where you can easily while away a day snapping photos or just hanging out.

how to get there:

By bus: Take bus to Westport; hostel is near terminal.
By car: Call hostel for directions.
By train: From Westport Station, hostel is across street.

---

granary hostel

Westport, Co. Mayo

Phone Number: 098–25903
Fax: 098–25903
Rates: €10 per person (about $10 US)
Private/family rooms: None
Kitchen available: Yes
Season: April 1 to September 30
Affiliation: None
Extras: Garden, meals ($), laundry

Insiders' tip:
Molloy's pub is great

Party index:

Not much to report here. Obviously this used to be a granary, and now the stone building holds a hostel interesting mostly for its outdoor showers and loos.

You're pretty close to the now somewhat tacky Westport House, a popular tourist draw.

how to get there:

By bus: Call hostel for transit route.
By car: Call hostel for directions.
By train: Call hostel for transit route.

---

old mill hostel

Barrack Yard, James Street, Westport, Co. Mayo

Phone Number: 098–25657
Fax: 098–28640
E-mail: oldmill@iol.ie
Rates: €13–€14 per person (about $13–$14 US); doubles €26–€30 (about

$26–$30 US)
Credit cards: Yes
Beds: 52
Private/family rooms: 1
Office hours: 8:00 A.M. to 11:00 P.M.
Season: January 4 to December 23
Affiliation: IHH, IHO
Extras: Laundry, bike rentals

This relatively new hostel, in an old eighteenth-century warehouse and mill area is a good place right in the center of town. It used to be a brewery but now supplies more decent beds in Westport.

Party index:

It comes equipped with a laundry and bicycles for hire, and there's also one private room to scramble for. For fun, walk beside the river beneath the trees.

how to get there:

By bus: From bus stop, walk to monument and then down James Street; hostel is on left.
By car: Call hostel for directions.
By train: Call hostel for transit route.

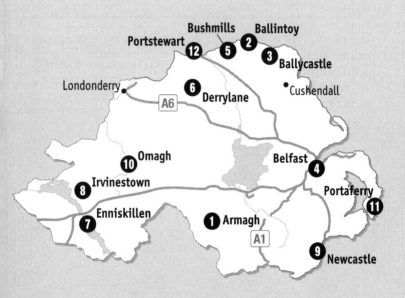

northern ireland

You'll hear good and bad stuff about Northern Ireland. The bad, of course, you've seen on the evening news. The good, well, that's less publicized—but this is an incredibly gorgeous land of sea cliffs, farms, and nice squares in small, manageable cities. The hostels here are almost all uniformly good, the people are very friendly, and the roads—well, if you've just come from Ireland, you'll be in for a pleasant treat.

To get here, you can take a ferry from Scotland or Wales. Or board a special bus that includes your ferry fare with the cost of the ticket.

armagh hostel

39 Abbey Street, Armagh, Co. Armagh BT61 1EB

Phone Number: 028–3751–1800
Fax: 028–3751–1801
E-mail: info@hini.org.uk
Rates: £12–£14 per HI member (about $18–$21 US)
Credit cards: Yes
Beds: 64
Private/family rooms: Yes
Kitchen available: Yes
Office hours: 8:00 to 11:00 A.M.; 5:00 P.M. to midnight
Season: January 2 to December 23
Affiliation: HINI
Extras: TV, bureau de change, bike rentals, meals, laundry, bar

We've learned great things about this hostel. All the rooms here are doubles or quads (save one six-bed room), which is terrific news, and all contain en-suite bathrooms, too. Double rooms even have TVs, hairdryers, and coffeemakers! Other services include bikes for rent and a money exchanging desk; the common room, of course, has a television. Kudos for disabled access as well.

Gestalt: Call to Armagh
Party index: 🎉🎉

Armagh itself, though troubled in recent decades because it's on the border of Ireland and Northern Ireland, is a decent place to stop over. The city has a beautiful mall—not the kind where you shop, but rather a beautiful green area surrounded by trees, perfect for Frisbee playing or sitting or whatever else.

how to get there:

By bus: Bus station is 250 yards from hostel.
By car: Call hostel for directions.
By train: Call hostel for transit route.

sheep island view hostel

42A Main Street, Ballintoy, Ballycastle, Co. Antrim BT546 LX

Phone Number: 028–207–69391
Fax: 028–207–69994
E-mail: sheepisland@hotmail.com
Rates: £10 per person (about $15 US); doubles £20 (about $30 US)
Credit cards: Yes
Beds: 60
Private/family rooms: 4
Affiliation: IHH
Extras: Meals ($), camping, laundry, bike rentals, free pickups

This IHH-affiliated joint is pretty new and was recently expanded. It's well placed on the wild northern coast of Northern Ireland, and early reports say it's a decent place.

Gestalt: Sheepish
Party index: 🎉🎉

Besides the dorms, there are four private rooms here, a campground, a laundry, and some bikes for hire.

how to get there:

By bus: Call hostel for pickup.
By car: Call hostel for directions.
By train: Call hostel for transit route.

whitepark bay hostel

157 Whitepark Road, Ballintoy, Ballycastle, Co. Antrim BT54 6NH

Phone Number: 028–207–31745
Fax: 028–207–32034
Rates: £10–£13 per person (about $15–$20 US)
Credit cards: Yes
Beds: 54
Family/private rooms: Yes
Kitchen available: Yes

Office hours: Call for hours.
Season: January to February, Friday to Sunday only; March to December 23, daily
Affiliation: HINI
Extras: Bike rentals, meals ($), conference room, TV, bureau de change, tours, activities, laundry, luggage storage

This newly fixed up facility is the creme de la creme of Northern Irish hostelling. If you're bringing the family or are just starting out as a hosteller, it's a good place to get your feet wet—about as luxurious as a hostel can be, though predictably bland.

Rooms consist of ten quad rooms, four doubles with TVs, and one six-bed dorm—all of which have en-suite bathroom facilities. The private rooms even have televisions in them. Coming with a group? Check out the conference rooms. Short of cash? There's a currency exchange desk here, too.

For fun, the staff sometimes organizes pub crawls and pony rides in the area and always rents out bicycles. Nearby, there's a great mile-long sandy beach that's rarely used. All in all, it's hard to go wrong.

Gestalt: Great Whitepark
Party index:

how to get there:

By bus: Bus stops 200 yards from hostel; call hostel for transit route.

By car: Take A2 6 miles west of Ballycastle; turn off at sign for Whitepark Bay, continue 150 yards to hostel.

By train: Portrush Station (12 miles away) and Coleraine Station (17 miles) are the closest.

castle hostel

62 Quay Road, Ballycastle, Co. Antrim BT546 LX

Phone Number: 028–207–62337
Rates: £7.50 per person (about $11.00 US); doubles £18 (about $27 US)
Beds: 30
Private/family rooms: 2

Affiliation: IHH
Extras: Laundry facilities

Gestalt: Bally up
Cleanliness:
Party Index:

Plenty of room here in Ballycastle, where this thirty-bed facility doesn't ever seem to fill up. It's spic-'n'-span clean, has two private rooms and a laundry, and is wheelchair accessible.

how to get there:

By bus: Call hostel for transit route.
By car: Call hostel for directions.
By train: Call hostel for transit route.

belfast

Despite a recent resurgence of "the Troubles," Belfast remains a fascinating visit—a peek into the real character of Northern Ireland. Just take good care to avoid a certain few neighborhoods where violence has periodically erupted.

belfast hostels
at a glance

HOSTEL	RATING	COST	IN A WORD	PAGE
Linen House		£6.50–£10.00	friendly	208
Arnie's Backpackers		£7.00–£9.50	comfy	206
The Ark		£8.50–£9.50	decent	206
Belfast International		£12.00–£13.00	iffy	207

the ark hostel

18 University Street, Belfast, Co. Antrim BT71 F2

Phone Number: 02890–329–626
Rates: £8.50–£9.50 per person (about $13–$14 US); doubles £32 (about $48 US)
Beds: 24
Private/family rooms: Yes
Kitchen available: Yes
Affiliation: None
Extras: Laundry, bike rentals, Internet access, tours, luggage storage, Internet access ($)

Gestalt: Central Ark
Cleanliness:
Hospitality:
Party index:

Accommodations at this Belfast joint include bunks in four- and eight-bed dorms plus three private rooms, and the hostel staff maintains a laundry and rents out bikes. Worth checking into.

how to get there:

By bus: Call hostel for transit route.
By car: Call hostel for directions.
By ferry: Call hostel for transit route.
By train: Call hostel for transit route.

arnie's backpackers hostel

63 Fitzwilliam Street, Belfast, Co. Antrim BT9 6AX

Phone Number: 02890–24867
Rates: £7.00–£9.00 per person (about $10.50–$14.00 US); doubles £24–£30 (about $36–$45 US)
Beds: 22
Private/family rooms: None
Kitchen available: Yes
Affiliation: IHH
Extras: TV, fireplace, laundry, bike rentals, Internet access

Popular, sociable, small, and comfortable: That describes Arnie's, which is less ragamuffin and more tasteful than you might have

expected. Dormitories are good, there's a fireplace and television in the common room, and the kitchen's kept surprisingly orderly. Queen's University is nearby, if you need the culture. There are no private rooms here, however.

Gestalt: Arnie's Army
Party index:

how to get there:

By bus: Take 70 or 71 bus to hostel.
By car: Call hostel for directions.
By ferry: Call hostel for transit route.
By train: Call hostel for transit route.

belfast international hostel

22-32 Donegal Road, Belfast, Co. Antrim BT12 5JN

Phone Number: 028–9031–5435
Fax: 028–9043–9699
E-mail: info@hini.org.uk
Rates: £12.00–£13.00 per HI member (about $18.00–$19.50 US)
Credit cards: Yes
Beds: 120
Family/private rooms: Yes
Kitchen available: No
Office hours: Twenty-four hours
Affiliation: HINI
Extras: Laundry, meals ($), TV, bike rentals, car rental discounts, bike storage, bar, coffee shop, Internet access

This HINI hostel is a big concrete block of a building—generally blah and not in the best neighborhood of downtown, so we'd look at the two smaller places in town as possible alternatives. Also, there's no kitchen. Say what?? You gotta be kidding. We appreciate the fact that this hostel was purpose-built, but geez.

Anyway, the place is as institutional and sterile as a hospital, though most

Insiders' tip:
Good bus tours of city

Gestalt: Not so Belfast

Cleanliness:

Party index:

rooms are doubles (sixteen of 'em) or quads (nineteen of those), so that's cool. It's quite clean, of course, and has a decent cafeteria and laundry. The huge common room is dominated by the TV, unfortunately.

The area can be dodgy at night—actually, violence has occurred here during the daytime, too. It's a touchy place during summertime parades that flare the tension between Protestants and Catholics, and hostellers could come into the line of fire. That's not exactly the kind of culture we were wanting to get.

how to get there:

By bus: From bus station take 89 or 90 bus to hostel; from downtown take 69, 70, or 71 bus to hostel.
By car: Call hostel for directions.
By train: Central Station is 3 miles away.

linen house hostel
(paddy's backpackers)

18-20 Kent Street, Belfast BT1 2JA

Phone Number: 02890–586–400
Fax: 02890–586–444
E-mail: info@belfasthostel.com
Rates: £6.50–£10.00 (about $8.00–$15.00 US); doubles £24–£30 (about $36–$45 US)
Credit cards: None
Beds: 130
Family/private rooms: Sometimes
Affiliation: IHH
Extras: Meals ($), laundry

Located in Belfast's cathedral quarter, this hostel was carved out of a converted factory. It's extremely central, near all transit services and the main sights of town.

In summer it's made up of six-to-eight-bed dorms with shared bathrooms, an eight-bed dorm with its own bathroom, and a big eighteen-bed room that's a mixture of guys and gals. That might not be your cup of tea if you value privacy. In the off-season, things relax a little and some double rooms become available.

Gestalt: Paddy-o
Hospitality:
Party index:

how to get there:

By bus: Contact hostel for transit route.
By car: Contact hostel for directions.
By train: Contact hostel for transit route.

mill rest hostel

49 Main Street, Bushmills, Co. Antrim BT57 8QA

Phone Number: 028–2073–1222
Fax Number: 028–2073–0493
Rates: £10–£12 per HI member (about $15 to $18 US)
Beds: Contact hostel for current number.
Private/family rooms: Yes
Kitchen available: Yes
Office hours: Call for hours
Season: January 2 to December 23
Affiliation: HINI
Extras: Conference room, laundry, bike storage, fireplace, meals ($)

This new HINI hostel, right in tiny Bushmills, is supremely located for access to the nearby—and amazing—Giant's Causeway. It's especially good for families (some of the private rooms resemble lofts or studio apartments rather than bunkrooms).

There's a double room, a triple, thirteen quads, and five- and six-bed dormitory rooms to choose from. Each of these rooms has its own en-suite bathroom. The hostel restaurant serves break-

Party index:

fast and dinner, and the open lobby and dining area get high marks from hostellers in the know.

When you're not gaping at the rock formations in the causeway, you'll want to check out the village's singular attraction: a distillery where they've been cranking out whiskey since, oh, around 1600. It's a cheap date or rainy-day outing, especially given the fact that your £4 ticket gets you a free sample of the good stuff at the end.

how to get there:

By bus: Bus stops 50 yards from hostel. Contact hostel for transit route.

By car: Take A2 (Antrim Coast Road) to a point 2 miles south of Giants Causeway, just before central square in Bushmills.

By train: Portrush station, 5 miles away.

flax-mill hostel

Mill Lane, Derrylane, Dungiven, Co. Derry BT47

Phone Number: 028777–42655
Rates: £5.80 per person (about $9.00 US); doubles £11.60 (about $18.00 US)
Beds: 16
Private/family rooms: Yes
Affiliation: IHH
Extras: Camping, laundry, bike rentals, fireplace, free pickups

This old stone cottage—tucked in the woods not far from Derry City—

Gestalt: Just the flax
Hospitality:
Party index:

is something else: It's powered by gas, candles, an open fireplace, and a peat-fired boiler instead of electricity and offers a throwback from modern living. The wonderful owners used to serve delicious meals, but check ahead—that practice may have been discontinued. There are still two nice private rooms, however, and a friendly pub nearby. A great place to kick back from frantic traveling.

how to get there:

By bus: Call hostel for pickup.
By car: Call hostel for directions.
By train: Call hostel for transit route.

the bridges hostel

Belmore Street, Enniskillen, Co. Fermanagh BT74 6AA

Phone Number: 028–6634–0110
Fax Number: 028–6634–6873
Rates: £10–£12 per HI member (about $15–$18 US)
Private/family rooms: Yes
Kitchen available: Yes

Office hours: Call for hours
Season: January 2 to December 23
Affiliation: HINI
Extras: Restaurant, laundry, bike storage, Internet access, TV lounge

A hostel affiliated with Bill Clinton?? Well . . . sort of.

This new HINI hostel is located in war-torn Enniskillen, a town notorious throughout Ireland and the North for the bomb that ripped through (in U2 singer Bono's words) "a parade of old-age pensioners"; that date in 1987 is now and forever known as "Sunday Bloody Sunday".

The William Jefferson Clinton International Peace Centre, of which this hostel is part, works to create understanding between divergent points of view; hence the name "Bridges". It was also built with the natural environment in mind—it's got solar panels and a whole lot of other ecological bells and whistles.

Everything's new here, and thus modern and top-flight. Accommodations consist of six double rooms, thirteen quad rooms, and a six-bed dorm; each room has its own bathroom.

Party index: 🎉🎉

The television room is popular, as is the kitchen.

For fun, hit a pub, check out the local castle, strike out for one of the many pretty lakes, parks, and caves in the surrounding area—or just sit back and contemplate the bitter history between Protestant and Catholic that played out here one terrible day in 1987.

how to get there:

By bus: Bus stops on Sligo Road, ⅓ mile from hostel. Contact hostel for transit details.

By car: Contact hostel for directions.

By train: Nearest station is in Sligo, 45 miles away.

castle archdale hostel

Irvinestown, Co. Fermanagh BT94 1PP

Phone Number: 028686–28118
Rates: £6.50–£7.50 per HI member (about $10.00–$11.00 US)
Credit cards: Yes
Beds: 55

Family/private rooms: Yes
Kitchen available: Yes
Season: March 1 to October 31
Affiliation: HINI
Extras: Bike rentals, TV, laundry

About 10 miles north of pretty Enniskillen, this hostel—in a building built in 1773—sits in a county park fronting the shores of quiet Lough Erne (and, no, that's not Lough Ernie).

Accommodations consist of one quad room, one six-bed dorm room, and two huge dorms in the eighteenth-century house. They'll rent you a bike for trolling around, and there's a television in the common room if you really need one.

Gestalt: Arch angel
Party Index: 🎉🎉

how to get there:

By bus: From Enniskillen take Pettigo bus to Lisnarick and walk 2 miles to hostel. Or take 194 bus to park.

By car: From Enniskillen take B82 for 11 miles north. Hostel is in park.

By train: Kesh Station is 2 miles away.

key to icons

 Attractive natural setting

 Comfortable beds

 Good for active travelers

 Ecologically aware hostel

 A particularly good value

 Visual arts at hostel or nearby

 Superior kitchen facilities or cafe

 Wheelchair accessible

 Music at hostel or nearby

 Offbeat or eccentric place

 Good for business travelers

 Great hostel for skiers

 Superior bathroom facilities

 Especially well suited for families

 Bar or pub at hostel or nearby

 Romantic private rooms

 Editors' choice: among our very favorite hostels

newcastle hostel

30 Downs Road, Newcastle, Co. Down BT33 0AG

Phone Number: 028–4372–2133
Fax: 028–4372–2133
Rates: £9–£10 per HI member (about $14–$15 US)
Credit cards: Yes
Beds: 40
Private/family rooms: Yes
Kitchen available: Yes
Season: March 1 to December 23
Affiliation: HINI
Extras: Laundry, TV, bike storage

This hostel, located on the ocean in the "other" Newcastle, is a strangely decorated old home, but it's nice to see a little change after all the drab

Gestalt: New order
Party index: 🎉🎉

hostels throughout the U.K. and Ireland. (Our only question: Was the wackily retro look here intentional or born of necessity? You decide.) Dorms consist of six- and seven-bed rooms, plus one quad and a special "family annex."

how to get there:

By bus: From bus station walk 150 yards to hostel.
By car: Call hostel for directions.
By train: From train station walk 1 mile to hostel.

omagh independent hostel

9A Waterworks Road, Omagh, Co. Tyrone BT79 7JS

Phone Number: 02882–241–973
Fax: 02882–241–973
Rates: £8 per person (about $12 US); doubles £20 (about $30 US)
Beds: 27
Private/family rooms: 2
Season: March 1 to December 1

Affiliation: IHH
Extras: Camping, laundry, bike rentals, free pickups

Nice place here, with an emphasis on getting out into the fresh Northern Irish air—even when that air's a little soggy. They rent bikes here, maintain a campground and laundry, and have two private rooms.

Gestalt: Omagh goodness
Party index: 🎉🎉

how to get there:

By bus: From station walk along Mountjoy Road to Killybrack Road; turn right, continue to hostel. Or call hostel for pickup.
By car: Call hostel for directions.
By train: Call hostel for transit route.

barholm hostel

11 The Strand, Portaferry, Co. Down BT22 1PS

Phone Number: 028427–29598
Fax: 028427–29698
Rates: £6.00–£11.50 per person (about $10.00–$12.00 US)
Beds: 42
Private/family rooms: Yes
Affiliation: None
Extras: Laundry, meeting room

Gestalt: Portaferry tale
Party index: 🎉🎉

This friendly joint is pretty good: an old house with excellent lake views, equipped with two dining rooms and a conference center. There are thirteen dorms in all sizes, including singles, doubles, and family rooms; some have their own en-suite bathrooms.

how to get there:

By bus: Bus stop 100 yards from hostel; from Belfast take 10 bus to Portaferry.

By car: Call hostel for directions.

By train: Belfast Central Station, 30 miles away, is the closest stop; call hostel for transit route.

rick's causeway coast hostel

4 Victoria Terrace, Atlantic Circle, Portstewart, Co. Derry BT55

Phone Number: 028–70833789
Fax: 028–70835314
Rates: £7.50 per person (about $11.00 US); doubles £18–£22 (about $27–$33 US)
Beds: 27
Private/family rooms: 3
Affiliation: IHH
Extras: Fireplace, laundry

Another HINI winner, this place is so well designed that it actually has baths and fireplaces. There's a laundry for your convenience, too, and the three private rooms are also nice.

Insiders' tip: Morelli's for ice cream

Gestalt: Coast office

Party index:

how to get there:

By bus: Call hostel for transit route.
By car: Call hostel for directions.
By train: Call hostel for transit route.

paul's
picks

THE BEST HOSTELS IN IRELAND

about the
author

Paul Karr is a prize-winning writer, writing coach, and author or co-author of more than three dozen travel guidebooks. He contributes regularly to magazines and writes screenplays when he's not traveling. He has also been twice named writer-in-residence by the National Parks Service. You can contact him directly by e-mailing him at

Atomev@aol.com.

help us keep this
guide up to date

Every effort has been made by the author and editors to make this guide as accurate and useful as possible. However, many things can change after a guide is published—establishments close, phone numbers change, facilities come under new management, etc.

We would love to hear from you concerning your experiences with this guide and how you feel it could be improved and kept up to date. While we may not be able to respond to all comments and suggestions, we'll take them to heart and we'll also make certain to share them with the author. Please send your comments and suggestions to the following address:

The Globe Pequot Press
Reader Response/Editorial Department
P.O. Box 480
Guilford, CT 06437

Or you may e-mail us at:

editorial@GlobePequot.com

Thanks for your input, and happy travels!